# RANDY SCOTLAND

# THE *CREATIVE* EDGE.

## INSIDE THE AD WARS

**VIKING**

VIKING
Published by the Penguin Group
Penguin Books Canada Ltd, 10 Alcorn Avenue, Toronto, Ontario, Canada M4V 3B2
Penguin Books Ltd, 27 Wrights Lane, London W8 5TZ, England
Viking Penguin, a division of Penguin Books USA Inc., 375 Hudson Street, New
York, New York 10014, U.S.A.
Penguin Books Australia Ltd, Ringwood, Victoria, Australia
Penguin Books (NZ) Ltd, 182-190 Wairau Road, Auckland 10, New Zealand

Penguin Books Ltd, Registered Offices: Harmondsworth, Middlesex, England

First published 1994

10 9 8 7 6 5 4 3 2 1

Printed and bound in Canada on acid free paper ∞

**Canadian Cataloguing in Publication Data**

Scotland, Randy, 1954–
  The creative edge

ISBN 0-670-85064-0

1. Vickers and Benson Ltd. 2. Advertising agencies—Canada. I. Title.

HF6181.V53S36 1994     338.7'616591'0971     C94-930002-0

# INTRODUCTION

A DVERTISING AGENCIES, once considered (and often derided as) the fat-cats of the business world, are facing gut-wrenching change. Some of that can be traced to the usual villain: the sorry state of the economy. When budget-obsessed advertisers cut back on the work they commission, agencies are quick to feel the effects on their bottom lines.

But there is more at play here than the expected contraction that accompanies a cyclical "correction" in the economy. If that were the case, agencies could simply ride out the tough times, knowing that prosperity would be theirs at the first sign of an upturn.

Were it that simple today. Most agency principals and industry watchers, myself included, believe something more profound is happening. And as the song says, "What it is ain't exactly clear." But few doubt that the agency business as we've come to know it is in the midst of a major transformation.

To what? Leaner and meaner, certainly. More efficient and less bureaucratic, most definitely. Beyond that, no one really knows. It is just that excitement of the unknown, that sense of unexplored possibilities, that makes this business, at this particular time, so compelling.

As a reporter who has followed the advertising sector since 1980, I was naturally intrigued by the drama of unfolding events. The question became how best to compress the scope of an industry into a couple of hundred pages. Obviously, I would need a tight focus.

The answer all but suggested itself. Why not look at the business through the eyes of one firm? It would give a structure to the story for those unfamiliar with the terrain. And, hopefully, make it a much more instructive, and entertaining, read.

That decided, it came down to candidates. It should be a large, multi-disciplinary firm, owned by Canadians, with a wide roster of interesting accounts. Ideally, the agency would represent the marketplace in micro-cosm. Its problems and opportunities would be illustrative of the industry's problems and opportunities.

The task was made easier by the shrinking roll of big, privately run agencies still doing business in Canada. If this book had been written a decade ago, there would have been a trove of likely prospects. But the buy-out binge in the 1980s reduced their numbers substantially. Many of the big names of Canadian advertising—McKim Advertising, Ronalds-Reynolds, Foster Advertising and MacLaren Advertising among them—were bought up by expansion-minded multinationals.

That left only a handful of contenders. Some were rejected because they were mostly regional operations, others because their areas of specialization didn't meet the criterion of being broadly based. But one agency did stand out. Vickers & Benson Advertising Ltd., a firm steeped both in the history of the industry and the country, met all of the qualifications. It is Canadian-owned, has service capabilities over a range of communications disciplines and has an excellent list of blue-chip clients who market such familiar household products as Big Macs, Gatorade, Heineken and Cap'n Crunch cereal.

The fact that the agency has also worked extensively with the Liberal Party of Canada is a bonus. Vickers & Benson has created ads that helped elect prime ministers, from Pierre Trudeau in the 1970s to Jean Chrétien in the 1990s.

The next big question was whether the agency would allow me to tell their tale. A book like the one I proposed would only work if the principals of Vickers & Benson permitted access to the inner sanctum. Otherwise, it would merely be a dry reiteration of faded press clippings and third-party gossip. Hardly the insider's insight I had hoped to gain.

From my experience on the beat, I knew that ad agencies are notoriously reticent about divulging company secrets. Their rationale is easy to understand. They are, after all, in business to supply a service to their clients. They are privy to top-secret information about new products, proprietary strategies and corporate goals. Clients pay handsomely to ensure confidentiality. Discretion is never optional.

With some trepidation, I set up an appointment to meet the top officers of the agency. I met with Terry O'Malley, the chairman, and John Hayter, president and chief executive officer. Also present were Jim Satterthwaite, the chief operating officer, and Terry Bell, then the director of creative services.

Over sandwiches and soft drinks, we talked about the book. I explained that it was meant to provide a fly-on-the-wall perspective of the agency. That it would examine the processes of the advertising craft. I was more interested in the way ads were produced, I told them, than innuendo. The goal, quite simply, was to show the workings of a big-city agency and how it was coping with the vagaries of an industry in transition.

The admen listened to my spiel, then peppered me with questions.

What about clients? How much would I reveal about them? Would I write about everything I saw, warts and all? Would people even be interested in a book about an ad agency?

I tried to answer the best I could. Yes, I would write about clients, and yes, I intended to depict as accurately as possible what I observed. However, I reassured them that this was not to be some sensational potboiler. They would have to trust me not to divulge information that would irresponsibly harm the agency's prospects and profile.

They thanked me for considering them, said they would talk it over and get back to me. A few days later, Hayter called to say that they, with one proviso, would co-operate. I was to respect their wishes on the rare occasions something was deemed off the record. In return, they would grant access to meetings, memos and members of staff as I saw fit.

I agreed with the stipulation, taking Hayter at his word that he would not capriciously invoke confidentiality. My trust in him has been richly rewarded. The only time he did request I close my notebook was when he and the rest of the agency's senior executives were discussing budgets and finances. Their reasoning was straightforward: Vickers & Benson is a privately held company and no one—besides its shareholders, accountant and, of course, the tax man—need know those particulars.

For that reason, I have only included financial information that is already on the public record. I do not believe this in any way diminishes the telling of the story.

It was one of those serendipitous strokes of fortune that I was present just as the agency was undergoing a major corporate upheaval. Like other agencies its size, Vickers & Benson was grappling with a marketplace in turmoil, as advertisers looked for better, faster and more accountable action from their agency partners.

The heart of this book is concerned with Vickers & Benson's unique response to those demands. Whether it is an answer applicable to all ad agencies is a moot point. Time will tell if the course they have chosen is the right one.

The time frame of this book covers a period from December 1992 through January 1994.

# Acknowledgments

I HAVE MANY PEOPLE to thank for their assistance in making this book possible.

First and foremost, I owe a great debt of gratitude to the men and women of Vickers & Benson, who were unfailingly helpful and kind. In particular, I would like to acknowledge the many hours granted me by John Hayter, Terry O'Malley, Jim Satterthwaite, Terry Bell, Bruce Philp, Larry Gordon, Joe Warwick, Mike McCormick, John Boniface, Bruce Claassen, Richard Cousineau and Sue Kirkwood. A special tip of my hat to Nadia Ostapchuk, Hayter's executive secretary.

Thanks also to Senator Keith Davey, who braved the worst storm of the winter of 1992 to meet with me; and to management consultant David Hurst, who was generous with both his time and insights.

I would like to thank the editors at *The Financial Post* for their encouragement and support, especially Araminta Wordsworth and Jaimie Hubbard.

Grateful acknowledgment is made to Wayne Gooding, editor of *Marketing*, for allowing me access to the magazine's files. Heartfelt thanks are also due to Gooding's award-winning predecessor, Colin Muncie, who hired me in 1980 as a junior reporter and who introduced me to the world of advertising. I would also like to thank Mark Smyka, editor of *Strategy* and a former co-worker, for helping me understand that world. I learned by following his example.

Thanks also to Vic Humphreys, former editor of *Oilweek* magazine in Calgary, who gave me my start in journalism; and to Alistair MacLeod, my creative-writing professor at the University of Windsor, who helped hone my craft.

I must also acknowledge Cynthia Good, my publisher at Penguin, for the words of encouragement and sound advice.

Thank you to my parents, Jack and Eloise Scotland of Calgary, for their unflagging support, and to Garry, Dave ("Laurie"), Robin and Rosanne and their families. A special thank-you to the Reverend John L. Pottruff, my late grandfather, for instilling the love of words.

I would also like to thank my other "family," my many friends who over the years have indulged my idiosyncrasies with love and under-standing: Judy Roberts and Don Bruce of Alert Bay, British Columbia; Dale Larsen and Eleanor Crilly of Ojai, California; Craig Ponton, and Cindy and Gary Imler of Calgary; Brad Lumley and Tony Ward of St. Thomas, Ontario; Leslie C. Smith, Glenn Robinson, Jim Gale, Tony Farebrother, Heather Ramsay, Geoffrey Paterson, Barb and Richard Day, Thelma Burns and Tara, of Toronto.

Thank you, too, to Phil Burns, whose *Webster's* proved invaluable.

And the biggest thank-you of all to Robin Burns, to whom this book is dedicated, for love and support beyond the call of duty.

# THE *CREATIVE* EDGE.

# CHAPTER 1

A N ADVERTISING AGENCY is a lot like one of those manic late-night TV commercials played on an endless, maddening loop; an ampheta-mine-paced world of blurring voices and people on the edge.

Vickers & Benson Advertising Ltd. is no exception.

Walk down one corridor and bump into an impromptu meeting of black-jeaned copywriters hotly debating the music track for a radio spot desperately close to deadline.

Round another corner and two account executives in designer suits are swapping horror stories about The Client From Hell.

One floor down, a strategy session is in full swing as a management team tries to figure out how to get on the short list for a major account that's come up for grabs.

Across the hall, the direct-marketing department is putting the finishing touches on a big-budget mail program for Ford Canada, and the promotion people are briefing the actor who plays Ronald McDonald on the day's itinerary of personal appearances.

The research chief is handed a confidential dossier on Molson Breweries—and asked to report his findings by next week.

The president is schmoozing a major client in one boardroom, while the executive art director ponders a photographer's portfolio in another. A creative team has found a quiet corner to brainstorm a concept for a Heineken campaign that's had them stymied for the last two days.

A steady stream of clients, suppliers, media representatives and salesmen present themselves at the main reception desk. By day's end their names will have filled page after page in the log book. Bicycle couriers in torn spandex and fingerless gloves arrive to pick up page proofs for approval, returning with rough cuts of a commercial from a production studio across town.

Phones clatter everywhere. Fax machines spit out their endless reams. Computer keys click-clack in counterpoint.

Just a typical morning in the downtown Toronto offices of one of Canada's oldest and largest ad firms, behind whose walls are dreamt the siren images that seduce us to buy, buy, buy. It is here that the consumer psyche is massaged and prodded, tempted and teased. Where the icons of commercial culture are fashioned, flickering to life in the nation's living rooms.

Like most agencies, Vickers & Benson's route to the final product is rarely linear. At any given time dozens of projects are on the go, all in various stages of completion.

For every commercial on the air, there are many more undergoing pre-campaign research, or focus-group testing, or stuck in limbo as a client decides if a particular line of copy needs sharpening—or whether it even needs to be there at all.

For each TV spot, there may be corresponding radio commercials, print ads, billboards, direct-mail pieces, public-relations activities, sponsored events, contests, coupons and other such marketing gambits in simultaneous development.

Remarkably, all these tasks are performed by only a couple hundred people, whose job skills must include the ability to juggle a sometimes frantic workload.

Follow a creative director for a day. It begins early. An 8:00 a.m. casting call to find the right "face" to grace a new beer ad. A 9:30 meeting to discuss the first assignment for a new client. A working lunch to finalize the media plans for a magazine campaign in Western Canada.

At 1:30, a get-together of department heads to fix the strategy for that client pitch now just three weeks away. Then a few stolen minutes to make some hasty return phone calls. At 4:00, race down the street to supervise the editing of an anti-smoking commercial. Back to the office by 6:00. Time to mull over a few ideas for a radio spot due to begin production in four days. Then over to the neighbourhood bar for a couple of beers with a reporter doing a story on sex-role stereotyping in the advertising business.

The whole process is repeated the next day with new assignments, deadlier deadlines.

It's the same for other V&Bers. A dedicated few are in their offices by dawn. Lights still burn as midnight nears. Time loses all meaning when a big presentation is imminent, forcing the pitch team into hyperdrive to finish a project that would normally take weeks to polish. Weekends are awash in bottomless cups of coffee, take-out pizza and beer.

And on top of everything else, there are the meetings—a seemingly inexhaustible supply of think tanks, strategy sessions and client briefings. There are even meetings to discuss the number of meetings keeping staff from their work.

There are compensations, of course. V&Bers are generally well paid for their efforts. Once they advance beyond junior positions, salaries climb precipitously. Six-figure remunerations are standard in the top echelons.

And there are less tangible, but equally rewarding, benefits. Chief among them is the relative freedom working in an agency provides. It is, after all, an artistic profession, one that is peopled with individualists, a few oddballs and an exuberant mix of wunderkinder.

The usual restrictions of the workplace are relaxed, even suspended, especially in the creative department. Corporate dress codes are less formal. Offices reflect the idiosyncrasies of their owners, with oddball assortments of posters, advertising bric-a-brac and souvenirs of past campaigns adorning walls and desks. Laughter floats down hallways, mixing with the loud rock 'n' roll of a new commercial blasting from a presentation room.

The cliché has it that advertising is a young man's—and increasingly, woman's—profession. There is truth to that at Vickers & Benson. Except for senior executives, the bulk of the staff are young, most in their twenties and thirties. By the time they reach middle age, most will have left the agency, started their own firms or quit the business altogether. Only the really committed, and talented, will stick it out to retirement age.

That is unless they happen to have the unhappy luck of working on an account the agency loses. When big clients walk, positions and people are sacked as well. No agency, not even a big one like Vickers & Benson, can keep idle staff on the payroll during times of restraint.

The relentless pressure frazzles even the level-headed. Rivalry splits ranks, and tempers flare over minor slights. Competition for favour from superiors can be cut-throat.

It's that way in any big agency. You expect jealousy and tantrums in such a highly strung environment. But it goes beyond that at Vickers &

Benson. There is a darker, more disturbing force at work here; an undercurrent of suspicion and resentment that at first is hard to pin down because everyone is so damned polite, particularly to visitors. Appearances, after all, matter in the image-making business.

But strip away the surface civility and it becomes more and more obvious that Vickers & Benson is a house that is dangerously divided.

We must flip back the calendar to February 1991 to find out why.

Terry O'Malley, the chairman and the agency's largest shareholder, has just hired John Hayter as president, chief executive officer and heir apparent. It is a reluctant choice. Not that he doesn't like the man. It's just that he's not sure he wants to give up control. At least, not quite yet.

He sees himself as the custodian of Vickers & Benson's reputation; one that, in an industry known for its back-stabbing ruthlessness, is respected for its gentlemanly code of ethics, its old-school sense of fair play. He is the father figure who upholds those values and virtues. Who nurtures—even coddles—an extended family of idolizing employees.

But O'Malley doesn't know if he has the stamina or desire to stay the course. The economy is in recession, major clients are growing restless, and Vickers & Benson is barely breaking even. After thirty years in the ad wars, he is tired and more than a little despondent.

Bill Bremner, his long-time partner who is anxious to retire and cash in his shares, finally coaxes O'Malley to action. Hayter is brought in, and with him the start of a new order.

O'Malley retreats to his office to brood. He wonders if he has made the right decision. What now for Vickers & Benson? What next for him?

Meantime, Hayter is anxious to quash the status quo, to shake things up. He wants to get everyone working as a team, land more business, win more awards. To turn up the dial.

Family is important, but so is survival. If Vickers & Benson is to remain viable in an increasingly hostile market-place, quick changes and tough choices will have to be made.

The need to sharpen the focus, to get aggressive, is urgent. As a privately owned agency, Vickers & Benson will have to be smarter and act faster than the multinational shops that are increasingly dominating the business.

As an independent, the agency cannot rely on accounts crossing borders the way rivals can. Hayter knows he will never pick up a phone to hear a superior in New York or London say because headquarters has won an international client, the Canadian assignment is automatically his. By the same token, neither will he ever be surprised to hear he has to forfeit an account because it conflicts with a piece of business held by an affiliate in Chicago or Sydney. Hayter cannot count on ready-made campaigns prepared by American or Spanish counterparts crossing into Canada with only a light touch-up here and minor adaptation there.

Every client Vickers & Benson has is won by its own hard work. Every piece of advertising is prepared by the agency's own people. There is no Los Angeles research department to consult. No Dallas creative stars who can be flown in to fix an account that is in trouble.

Hayter knows the agency needs help to realize his vision, so he hires a slate of lieutenants. A new chief operating officer, a new creative head, a new director of client services.

Predictably, schisms soon surface. The O'Malley loyalists, many of whom have spent years—and some of them decades—with the agency, clash with the newcomers. Not that there is open warfare. That isn't the V&B way. But the smiles are forced just the same. Everyone questions his neighbours' agendas and allegiances. Distrust and paranoia threaten to cripple the operation.

Hayter knows the two camps must come together or they will tear the agency apart. Already the buzz on the street has it that Vickers & Benson is in trouble. How long before clients pick up the scent and begin deserting? In the ad world, everyone shuns a loser. The merest whisper of trouble can spark a stampede out the door.

And what an ignoble end that would be for such a grand institution as Vickers & Benson, an agency whose ads have sold more Fords, more Big Macs, more Gatorade, more Bank of Montreal savings accounts, more Quaker Oats cereal, more Amstel beer than any other in Canada. That an agency which has even helped elect prime ministers should self-destruct is unthinkable.

But the agency has triumphed over adversity before. The Depression, World War II, the defeat of governments, the loss of huge accounts. Each time, Vickers & Benson bounced back. Its resilience is the stuff of advertising legend.

Vickers & Benson was founded in 1924, but its beginnings go back to 1918. That's when Rex Henry Vickers, then a dapper young man in his mid-twenties, marched into the Montreal art studio of Donald Fleetwood Benson.

Benson, who was a few years younger, was taken aback by his surprise guest. Sixty-five years later, he recalled that first meeting in an interview with the trade publication *Marketing* magazine: "[Vickers] was leaning on a cane, but not because he was lame. It went with his fashionable spats. He was a discharged army officer and he had just come down to Montreal from Ottawa."

Vickers introduced himself as an artist by trade with a proposition to make. He was looking for a place to live and to paint, but wanted some-body to split the costs. Would Benson be interested in sharing?

Benson, who was no stranger to need, said yes. The youngest of twelve children, he had quit school in grade seven to help support his family after the lumber business founded by his grandfather went broke. As a child, he sold flowers his mother grew in her garden. In his teens, he worked briefly in a bank.

Finally, he talked his way into McKim Advertising, Canada's oldest ad agency, founded in Montreal in 1889. He landed a job as a copywriter, even though he had never written a line of copy in his life.

Vickers was also attracted to the ad business. He found a job as an art director in the Montreal office of a small American firm.

In 1924, the two men decided to join forces and hang out their own shingle. Benson cashed in a three-hundred-dollar insurance policy, and Vickers kicked in another four hundred dollars. They flipped a coin to see who would be president. Vickers won, and Vickers & Benson Advertising Ltd. was open for business.

"It was a lean time, and we had to play it close to the chest," Vickers reminisced in a 1962 *Marketing* article. "We bought pencils two at a time. One for him and one for me. We worked the first ninety days, every day through Christmas and New Year's, until 11 p.m. We were creative men, and we learned the business side as we went along. And we played it safe. No wood panelling on the walls like today. The money went back in the business."

They survived by dint of hard work and trust in their gut instincts. "Today, all these so-called ad geniuses are babies," Vickers sniffed. "They have to have air conditioning, their coffee breaks and all that stuff. In the old days we were too happy to have a job to notice the heat."

Their little agency grew and prospered. They acquired an enviable list of clients, including Canada Starch Co., Frontenac Breweries, Seagram Distilleries Ltd., Ford Motor Co. of Canada, the Bank of Montreal and

Seven-Up Canada Inc. By 1931, it was time to expand, and Benson moved to Toronto to open a branch office. Vickers remained to rule the roost in Montreal.

Though separated, they maintained strong personal ties. In 1965, when they sold their interests in the agency, by then one of the largest in the country, to ten company directors, they had been partners for an extraordinary forty-one years. Vickers died the following year at age seventy-three.

"Vickers and Benson were two very close personal friends," Bryan Vaughan, who took over as president, remembers today. "They used to go hunting and fishing together."

Vaughan, now eighty, has especially fond memories of Benson. "He was extremely well liked," he says. That was true not only within the agency but in the larger Toronto business community as well. He belonged to all the right clubs, moved in the best circles.

"He was a very smart man. But in addition to that, he was a gentle man."

Vaughan and Benson were friends long before they became colleagues. It was only when Benson asked Vaughan, a successful public-relations man, to help out on some institutional ads the agency was preparing that they became business associates as well.

"He wanted somebody to sit in on his planning board," Vaughan says, "which I was happy to do, naturally. About eight or ten months later, he had to go into the hospital for a minor operation that he was told was only going to keep him away from the office for two or three days."

Benson asked him to take care of the place while he was away, and again Vaughan agreed.

"Unfortunately, he developed blood poisoning and other complications, and was off for several months. Meantime, the agency—and I guess I was largely responsible—got several big accounts. So he asked me if I would stay on as managing director."

A third time Vaughan agreed. He sold his PR firm, and joined Vickers & Benson as a salaried employee.

Although based in Toronto, he made regular trips to Montreal to work with Vickers.

"He, too, was a fine person, but very much an individualist. He didn't have any children unfortunately, although he had a lovely wife, as did Don Benson. I got along pretty well with him. From time to time he would call me down to help on a special presentation, things like that."

On one occasion it was to sit in on a briefing for Seagrams, one of Vickers' key accounts.

"He and Mr. Sam, as they called Sam Bronfman, were very good friends," Vaughan recalls. "And Sam Bronfman was a top-flight marketer. He always liked to sit in on advertising meetings.

"Anyway, we were making a presentation one day, and we were all set to go and we were waiting for him. He sent in word that he was going to be a little late, but to proceed. So I started off, and he sidled in and sat down at a chair at the back of the table.

"I paused and said, 'Mr. Sam, come on up and sit at the head of the table.' And he said, 'You goddamn son of a bitch! Wherever I sit is the head of the table!'"

Vaughan laughs heartily at the memory. "He had a lot of expletives which he used all the time. He really knew his stuff, though."

When the founders bowed out, there was none of the dislocation one expects with the transition of power. "It was almost imperceptible," Vaughan says, "and I think that's a tribute to them, because they were very generous in bringing people along. They were good mentors and they passed their clients along, introducing staff to the clients at social occasions and so on.

"They were great men. They were good business people, sure. But they recognized fundamentals that are equally important."

Vickers & Benson flourished during Vaughan's tenure. It moved from the bottom twenty of the country's largest agencies into the top five. It moved offices every few years, each time into a larger space to accommodate the expanding numbers of staff.

The agency had its share of growing pains along the way. Vaughan knew there was much work to do to get Vickers & Benson on the fast track.

One of the first things he did after becoming managing director was to jolt the agency's creative department from its lethargy. He tapped an old high-school buddy, Stan Furnival, who was then working at crosstown competitor Foster Advertising Ltd.

"My strength was being able to spot and slot the right people," Vaughan says. "[Furnival] was probably the most outstanding creative fellow in Canada at the time."

Furnival wasted no time in raiding Foster's creative department for recruits. He hired Terry O'Malley, a promising copywriter, who started at Vickers & Benson on Valentine's Day, 1964. The same year, O'Malley introduced Bill Bremner, a friend of his who worked on the account side at Foster, to Vaughan. Bremner switched over to Vickers & Benson on September 8.

O'Malley, who by that time had already done stints at two other agencies, talked about his Foster days in a 1975 article in *Marketing*.

"It was a wide-open agency which practised a sort of frontier-type advertising where everyone shot from the hip," he said. "Red Foster was president then and he made everything an occasion. We'd hear on a Tuesday that an account was up for grabs and by Wednesday we'd be ready with everything from TV commercials to sales promotional ideas."

O'Malley also related a story that has since become industry lore:

"Red had this painted box full of bits of folded paper and he'd plop it dramatically on the table after our presentation and say, 'Look, we not only have all those brilliant ideas we've just shown you, but we also have millions more in this box.' Then he'd stick his hand in and read three from the top of the pile. We'd all be sitting there sweating because we knew, and hoped he'd remember, that all the rest were just blank bits of folded paper."

What a culture shock to come from that off-the-wall environment to what was then a decidedly drab and staid Vickers & Benson. The same *Marketing* article paints a dismal picture:

"In its early stages, V&B was known as a competent agency with a boy-scout philosophy. But not much flair. It became hyper-innovative and aggressive under the influence of people like O'Malley and Bremner but, until fairly recently, lacked discipline and suffered from gaps in its overall strength (weak media and account services, for instance).

"Then around 1969/70 the agency ran into serious problems and lost about $5 million worth of billings. The advertising industry watched and waited for V&B to heave one last mighty groan and give up the ghost."

Bremner told the magazine the bad rap was warranted.

"O'Malley and I were looking over the Bank of Montreal account one night," he recalled. "It was about two in the morning when we came to the realization that we were in trouble on the account. We also knew that if Bank of Montreal went others were sure to follow. We subsequently watched in horror as the bank pulled out and the chain reaction set in."

When the Bank of Montreal, which had been a Vickers & Benson client for a quarter century (and which the agency won back in the

1980s), subsequently hired an American firm, it created a furore in the ad community. It was a scandalous move for a Canadian bank to make at a time when the country was still flushed with post-Centennial nationalist fervour.

"Despite the uproar...we knew we deserved to lose the account," Bremner said. "We'd allowed ourselves to become too detached. And there was a low point there when we'd lost such a lot of business when it would have been damned easy to throw in the towel. We didn't. We worked damned hard to get back on our feet and to make sure we learned the lessons inherent in our misfortune."

Not that the reviews were all bad. In fact, it was during this period that Vickers & Benson began developing an ability to perform a wide variety of communications tasks, now an industry standard. That wasn't so thirty years ago. Advertising agencies prepared ads. Period. But Vaughan insisted his people become proficient in a range of integrated marketing activities.

"That was one of my contributions," he boasts. "I believed in advertising, but I also believed in public relations and marketing. At the time, a lot of people in the business didn't have much use for public relations."

It was a time when most companies solved their marketing problems by simply producing another TV commercial or magazine campaign and bought as much media time and space as their budgets permitted.

By the cash-strapped 1990s, advertisers would no longer be able to afford to spend their troubles away. Consumers were more difficult to reach and win over. Increasingly, advertisers were exploring less costly, but more intrusive, solutions that went across a broad communications spectrum.

In this regard, Vickers & Benson was well placed. Even before it was trendy to do so, the agency had a banquet of services to tempt even the most demanding client.

If the agency was ahead of its time, it wasn't due to some divine inspiration or anticipation of where the industry was headed. To hear O'Malley tell it, Vickers & Benson became an integrated marketing firm almost by accident.

Back in the 1970s, there was no fashionable label to describe this kind of multi-disciplinary orientation. "We called it 'swarming,'" O'Malley deadpans.

And the cost to clients for all this attention and expertise? Zilch. The agency was throwing in all the extras for free. "We really hadn't figured out a way to charge for it," O'Malley admits, a bit sheepishly.

So while other agencies were just beginning to think about expanding their repertoire of services—and billing clients for the privilege—Vickers & Benson was simply offering the complete package at a one-stop price.

It was a naïve, and costly, way to operate. It meant that when the agency was doing work for Gulf Canada, one of its biggest clients in the 1970s, it would handle everything from preparing a coin-giveaway promotion to producing TV spots starring Johnny Wayne and Frank Shuster. It was just part of the Vickers & Benson way of doing business.

As it turned out, there was a silver lining to such magnanimity. The breadth of the agency's capabilities meant it was able to handle the diverse requirements of an advertiser as demanding as McDonald's Restaurants. By the late 1970s, Vickers & Benson could pitch the business with confidence. And win.

"The strengths of our people were broad," O'Malley says. "I kept saying there is no single answer to every problem. There are a variety of answers. Sometimes it takes four pieces to make one answer. I'm sure if we had been different kinds of people, and if money had been the motivation, we would have driven ourselves more to mass media. This 'depth' stuff is incredibly labour intensive. It's unbelievable. We devoted as much time designing tray-liners for McDonald's as we did doing a national ad."

But he wouldn't have had it any other way.

"I enjoy that kind of horizontal approach to the business, I guess. Maybe the answer is a promotional idea, or maybe it's a PR thing. And maybe we scrap everything and have an event. That was the advantage. You have this clean slate all the time to attack things, and try to keep the other guys off-guard. Come at them from different directions.

"From all directions."

After Vaughan's retirement in the mid-1970s, Bremner, as chairman, and O'Malley, as president and creative chief, assumed management and ownership control. Their ascension ushered in a prosperous period of largely proficient management, creative competence and steady growth.

Now skip ahead to 1985, a pivotal year for both Vickers & Benson and for the advertising world.

Don Benson is dead at the age of eighty-six, having spent his retirement years devoted to charitable work—he is past president of the Canadian Arthritis Society—and painting. He had lived to see the agency he co-founded with a handshake celebrate its sixtieth anniversary.

But 1985 is also the year the agency business went berserk. Vickers & Benson could not escape the madness, even if O'Malley and Bremner desperately wanted to.

The roller-coaster 1980s was a white-knuckle ride for every agency, large and small. Suddenly, Vickers & Benson and its brethren in the clubby Canadian ad community faced a new threat from abroad. The agency monoliths from the United States and Britain, intent on dominating the world advertising market, went on empire-building buy-out binges. Inevitably, they began moving in on the Canadians' turf.

Vickers & Benson, closely tied to the Liberal Party, had already suffered a major blow with the end of the Trudeau dynasty, and with it the loss of powerful friends in Ottawa and their lucrative ad contracts. Now to heighten the misery an onslaught of invaders was poised to attack.

O'Malley and Bremner watched with mounting alarm as one after another of their fellow Canadian agency-owners sold out to the Yanks and Brits.

The list read like a Who's Who of Canadian advertising, all firms founded by larger-than-life admen. Warren Reynolds. Red Foster. Jack MacLaren. Russell Kelley. James Lovick. Palmer Hayhurst. Anson McKim.

They were proud men, unabashedly Canadian, as were the men who took over the reins of the companies that bore their names. In the 1970s, a group of them even contemplated lobbying the federal government to enact protectionist legislation that would have made Canadian-content rules mandatory in the advertising business.

If such a law had been passed, foreign agencies would have been effectively shut out of the country. In the end, however, the admen backed off, fearing their actions would be interpreted as petty anti-Americanism.

Bremner, in a 1985 interview with *Marketing*, said he later had second thoughts about not pressing his friends in government to protect agencies like his.

"We felt that U.S. competition was healthy and that we could only get better by competing with their lead agencies," he said. "If we made one mistake, it was in not taking into consideration the fact that today it is easier for a U.S. agency to start up in Canada than it is for a Canadian to open up shop in New York.

"The multinationals have a great deal more money to front-end Canadian development as well as the ability to export U.S.-based accounts to Canada to help build their businesses. And with an open border, this becomes even more scary."

O'Malley, quoted in the same article, said he too underestimated the strength of the foreign juggernaut.

"I believe they have a psychological competitive edge because of the rub-off of the Madison Avenue image and the feeling that a U.S. agency in Canada provides a security blanket with their immense billings and supposed bench strength in New York.

"U.S. agencies are perceived to be more concerned and disciplined in their approach to the development of their clients' business. Intellect, discipline and a sense of urgency have nothing to do with the location of the agency's head office. It has to do with the intensity of the leadership of the agency, U.S. or Canadian. The talent bank is mostly Canadian anyway.

"The guy who works here today is no different the next day when he finds himself at a multinational agency. But suddenly, over there, he is a marketing expert, or a senior packaged-goods planner. A nondescript account man can suddenly become a strategist simply by walking across the street to an American agency."

The trickle of foreign agencies soon turned into a flood. At the beginning of the 1960s, there were only three foreign-owned agencies among Canada's top fifteen. By 1985, their numbers had swollen to eight. At the end of the decade, there were an even dozen. By the early 1990s, only one Canadian-owned agency, Quebec-based Cossette Communication-Marketing, remained in the top ten.

Like their peers, O'Malley and Bremner had also been courted by foreign interests with bulging wallets. But O'Malley, who had the largest stake in the company, resisted all blandishments, regardless of the temptation to take the money and run. He stubbornly insisted that Vickers & Benson and its blue-chip pedigree would stay Canadian, and it would remain employee-owned.

There seemed to be no end to the suitors, to the range of deals. Offers came from Europe, from America, from their own backyard. Morris Saffer, a maverick Toronto adman specializing in big retail accounts, came knocking. So did Madison Avenue's NW Ayer. One day over lunch Claude Lessard, president of Cossette, offered to write O'Malley a cheque on the spot.

There was even a offer to buy 50 per cent of the agency from leveraged buy-out artist and fellow Liberal stalwart Gerald Schwartz, the high-flying president of Toronto-based Onex Corporation.

"I am very strongly pro-Canadian," Schwartz said in 1988, when news of his interest in Vickers & Benson hit the street. "And I think there ought to be major Canadian-owned advertising agencies, and they are all disappearing. I think it's a tragedy.

"And if I can do anything to help Vickers & Benson—or frankly, anyone else that is a good business deal as well—retain its total Canadian ownership and sponsorship, I'd love to do it."

He professed an even more grandiose vision.

"If I were to invest in Vickers & Benson, one of the reasons would be to add some financial deep pockets to V&B so that they could create a home for any other agencies that are Canadian-owned and want to be part of a larger group. That would be terrific."

O'Malley tried to play down the story when the press picked up the scent. Embarrassed by the publicity, he said the deal was far from signed and sealed.

"Clients think we're selling the agency out from under them without even talking to them," he told *The Financial Times of Canada.* "I feel very defensive. It's like I've been seeing a girl for lunch, and everybody starts asking how pregnant she is."

That deal, like all the others before it, was not to be. O'Malley, seconded by Bremner, turned down each of them, some regretfully, but most with relief.

It wasn't until 1991 that a deal was struck with Hayter, a local lad who had made good on the international stage, first as the London-based managing director of Alberto-Culver, a heavyweight in the toiletry business, and then as the head of the Chicago office of Young & Rubicam, one of the world's largest ad agencies with offices around the world, including one in Toronto.

It was the Toronto office that had caused O'Malley and Bremner so much grief back in 1987, when out of the blue it scooped up one of Vickers & Benson's prized accounts, Ford Motor Company of Canada Ltd., a client for thirty-one years. It was a pivotal loss for the agency, and not only because it meant forfeiting $15 million in annual ad billings.

More important, it signalled that the old ways of doing business were finished, that the rules had changed. It meant the end of cozy and long-standing relationships, built on trust and sealed with a handshake. It didn't matter how good the work was—and Vickers & Benson's advertising for Ford was among the best in the automotive business—when decisions could be made from afar to terminate a contract for expediency's sake.

For Vickers & Benson, it was a rude welcome to a new cut-throat era, where the bottom line mattered more than corporate friendships, and a company's fate could be determined by a long-distance telephone call.

The account had simply dropped into Young & Rubicam's lap because someone in Ford's parent office in Dearborn, Michigan, decided the time was right to align its advertising with one agency north and south of the border.

Ford executives in Canada hadn't even met their counterparts at Young & Rubicam when the stunning news was announced on July 1. One chilling comment from Jack Glissold, Ford's vice-president of sales and marketing, rocked the Toronto advertising establishment: "We know who [Young & Rubicam's] accounts are—Labatt's and some others—but we really have very little knowledge of their people or their work."

O'Malley was enraged, and more than a little fearful. He believed that Ford's unilateral decision was "a tremendous message to Canadian agencies. It's going to be very, very difficult to compete because you just don't have the critical mass. If someone wanted to consider free trade in this industry—and this is the first clear look at it—you can see where we're going to stand."

Vickers & Benson later won back the carmaker's direct-marketing business. But that didn't ease the agony of losing the big advertising assignment. To this day, O'Malley still grieves.

How ironic, then, that four years later O'Malley and Bremner would ultimately agree to sell to a man who once held a top position with the very agency that had caused them such anguish.

But by that time their options were becoming more and more slim. Bremner was in poor health and wanted to retire. And O'Malley knew that Hayter was probably the best man to take over, to guide the agency into the next century.

At least he had a proven track record. And he was a Canadian. There would be no foreign masters, no need to change the company name with its blue-ribbon heritage.

And Hayter had been persistent. He had hounded Bremner and O'Malley relentlessly. The negotiations went on and on, month after month. It often looked as though an agreement had been reached, only to have the deal fall apart over one sticking point or another. After much jousting, the three men finally inked a deal in February 1991.

"Like everyone else in this business, I find it's a little tougher world than it was a few years ago, but the business [at Vickers & Benson] is solid," Hayter told the press. "It has a terrific list of blue-chip accounts, and many new relationships, which have excellent growth possibilities."

Hayter would become president and chief executive officer, and a major shareholder through a payback option. He would take over the duties of running the company's day-to-day operations. That would free up O'Malley to concentrate on his first love, writing advertising copy. Bremner could begin easing his way out of the company by taking on the honorific title of senior chairman, and with it a more sedate working schedule.

Unfortunately, his poor health prevented Bremner from enjoying the fruits of his labour. He died on May 2, 1993, of heart failure at his home in Uxbridge, Ontario. He was sixty-eight. He had been released from hospital only the day before, and had planned to marry his long-time companion, Maureen, the following week.

His colleagues, O'Malley in particular, were stunned by the loss. It was left to Joe Warwick, Vickers & Benson's jocular head of promotions, to write the obituary. It is a stirring and heartfelt tribute, with a dollop of self-serving boosterism thrown in for good measure. It also serves as a capsule history of the Bremner-O'Malley years:

[Bremner] joined the company in 1964 as an account supervisor following 12 years with the T. Eaton Company and Foster Advertising. He progressed through the ranks, becoming president in 1971 and chairman and chief executive officer in 1975.

Throughout his 28 years at V&B, Bill Bremner's vision and entrepreneurial style made him an industry leader and innovator who has left an indelible impression on the Canadian advertising community.

Mr. Bremner's success stemmed primarily from three strongly held convictions: his fierce pride in Canada; his belief in partners and employees; and his visionary understanding that to serve clients' best interests, marketing communications programs had to consist of more than just media advertising.

In 1967, with pride in our nation running at an all-time high, Bill Bremner volunteered his agency's services in the advertising and promotion of Canada's Centennial celebrations.

V&B broadcast producer John Lyons recalls Mr. Bremner championing the idea of a theme song for the Centennial. "Others thought it too nationalistic, I guess, but when Bobby Gimby came to us with his version of 'Canada,' Bill knew it was right and sold the idea at the highest level. The result was a tune that was whistled, hummed and sung by a whole generation of Canadians—a real source of spontaneous national pride."

His belief in Canada extended to Canadian institutions, specifically the Canadian advertising industry. Beginning in the 1960s, in competition with the powerful multinational agencies, Bill Bremner and his partner, Terrence O'Malley, built V&B into a communications powerhouse developing winning relationships with major clients such as Gulf Canada, the Dairy Bureau of Canada, the Ford Motor Company, H.J. Heinz, Bank of Montreal, Seagrams and McDonald's.

Mr. Bremner believed in his colleagues, instituting a system of broadly based employee shareholding that remains in effect today. He also understood, as indicated by V&B's long-time internal watchword: "The ad is just the beginning." At Mr. Bremner's direction,

Vickers & Benson became one of the first agencies to recognize the power of integrated communications by introducing business units dedicated to retail consulting, public relations, sales promotion, direct marketing and event marketing.

Industry colleague and market research specialist Martin Goldfarb said: "Bill treated advertising and marketing like a form of poetry. He believed that they reflected the values and mores of society. More important, he believed that thoughtful communications could lead those values in a very positive way. In that respect, Bill Bremner was my mentor, as well as the mentor of many leading figures in the advertising and marketing community."

Mr. Bremner enjoyed a lifetime passion for sports. As a participant, he starred in football at Vaughan Road Collegiate and the University of Toronto. He also played Inter-Collegiate and Senior B hockey. But his most significant contribution to sports was as a builder and volunteer. Through the years, he was a member of the Toronto Argonauts' Advisory Board; a founding member and director of the Canadian College Bowl (now the Vanier Cup); an innovator and special advisor to Team Canada '72; a director of the Canadian Professional Golfers' Association; and a shareholder in the Toronto Toros of the World Hockey Association.

In 1983, he was appointed by Ontario Premier William Davis as one of three members of the Ontario Stadium Study Committee, charged with recommending a site for the eventual SkyDome.

An active supporter of community causes, Mr. Bremner was an advisor and volunteer for such organizations as Variety Village, the Hospital for Sick Children, York University, the National Advertising Benevolent Society, Harbourfront and the Canadian Opera Company. In 1980, he was the recipient of the coveted "Promise of

Hope Award" presented for outstanding service on behalf of the Canadian Children's Foundation.

Mr. Bremner's devotion to co-workers, friends and family was noted by long-time partner and Vickers & Benson chairman, Terrence O'Malley. "Bill was everyone's uncle, he was everyone's ally, he was everyone's partner, and he hated to lose. He devoted his life to his family, his children and grandchildren. Nothing took precedence over that."

Immediately after he took control of the company, Hayter began bringing in his own hand-picked team. His first priority was to find someone to share the management load. Someone to become his partner and right-hand man. Someone he could trust.

Jim Satterthwaite fit the bill perfectly.

Hayter and Satterthwaite had first met twenty-five years earlier when the two worked in the Toronto office of New York agency giant J. Walter Thompson. Later their paths crossed again when Hayter, then London-bound with Alberto-Culver, recommended that Satterthwaite replace him in Canada.

Hayter had heard that his former colleague was available and figured he could sway him over to Vickers & Benson. His intuition was spot on. As it turned out, Satterthwaite was then casting about for exactly the kind of position Hayter was offering.

When Hayter called him about joining Vickers & Benson, Satterthwaite was at a crossroads. Hayter's offer to become Vickers & Benson's executive vice-president and chief operating officer was too good to turn down. He took out a loan, bought into the company and settled into a new role, thrilled that at last fortune was turning for the better.

The next move for Hayter was to hire someone to direct the agency's creative department, which by that point was in need of a shake-up. Once again, circumstances played in his favour.

As luck would have it, Terry Bell, a copywriter with a reputation for speaking his mind, was looking for gainful employment. Bell, who coincidentally got his start in advertising in the mailroom at Vickers & Benson in the 1960s, had just been fired from ad agency MacLaren:Lintas Inc. He had joined the firm only six weeks earlier.

His offence? Speaking to a *Globe and Mail* reporter, who was seeking a third-party opinion of a new television campaign for Canadian Airlines International Ltd., created by a rival agency, Chiat/Day Inc.

Bell was quoted as saying the spot was "fundamentally boring." A blunt assessment perhaps, but hardly extraordinary given the partisan nature of the agency business, where snipes at competitors are commonplace.

But what Bell didn't know was that the Edmonton affiliate of MacLaren:Lintas held a tiny portion of Canadian's advertising account. Bell's managers were aghast, believing his criticism, innocuous though it was, threatened the firm's place on the airline's agency roster.

The gossip on the street—never proven—was that officials at Canadian Airlines were demanding Bell's head. The damage-control experts at MacLaren:Lintas kicked into immediate action.

"We don't criticize other people's work," Bill Durnan, Bell's supervisor, said at the time of the firing. "Clients get uncomfortable about confidentiality and, I guess, the key word is discretion. We had to take a stand. It's just a matter of principle."

Bell felt betrayed. He didn't know the accounts the Edmonton office handled, and, besides, not one of his superiors had warned him it was against company policy to speak so openly to the press. He had, after all, informed Durnan and agency chief executive Tony Miller of the

*Globe*'s request for an interview. He had even invited them to sit in. They had declined.

So Bell found himself suddenly on his own, outraged at how he had been treated and wondering where he would go next, convinced his reputation had been irreparably scarred.

Meantime, the press began whipping up a storm of controversy that was to lead to Bell's exoneration.

*Marketing* magazine refused to let the story of his dismissal die. It canvassed agency presidents in Canada and abroad, asking them if they would have fired an employee for making similar comments about a competitor's work. Interestingly, the Canadians were divided on the issue. Some felt it was sometimes justifiable, others that it hampered the exchange of ideas so vital to a creative profession like advertising.

The foreign agency chiefs had no such qualms about what the pundits were calling "The Bell Affair." To a man they said they would not have fired him under those circumstances. One even said it should be a firing offence not to venture a frank assessment.

The resulting publicity did more for Bell's career than any number of awards could possibly achieve. He became a beacon for those who valued free speech above toeing the corporate line. Lionized by the press, he was the subject of countless debates in agency bars and boardrooms across the country.

In short, he was transformed into a hero, the very definition of integrity. Just the man Hayter needed to call attention to Vickers & Benson. He hoped that by hiring Bell the message would go out loud and clear that at one company, at least, individuality and outspokenness were welcome.

So both sides ended up getting what they desired. Hayter got his lightning rod, and Bell regained his dignity. He gratefully joined his alma mater as executive vice-president and director of creative services.

(Bell would try to avenge his dismissal from MacLaren:Lintas by hiring two of the agency's creative stars, art director Michael McLaughlin and copywriter Stephen Creet, best known for their award-winning work on Molson Canadian's "What Beer's All About" campaign. After negotiating a deal in the fall of 1992, and satisfied all the arrangements were in place, Bell took off for a European holiday. When he returned, he was flabbergasted to read in the trade press that his superstar recruits had outfoxed him by taking jobs at rival agency McKim Baker Lovick/BBDO. The betrayal was only alleviated when Bell later wooed Larry Gordon, his former art director partner at MacLaren:Lintas, into joining him at Vickers & Benson.)

Before his truncated stint at MacLaren:Lintas, Bell worked at the Toronto office of Saatchi & Saatchi Co., the London-based conglomerate founded by two enignmatic brothers, Charles and Maurice. More than any others in the topsy-turvy advertising world of the 1980s, the Saatchis were responsible for promoting the idea, and the ideal, of global marketing.

Their game plan was simplicity itself: Convince multinational advertisers that the world was merely one huge market-place, and that consumers everywhere shared the same basic desires and aspirations, regardless of language, custom or politics. It therefore followed that the same advertising campaign could play equally well in Moscow, Manchester and Moose Jaw.

And if only one campaign could do the trick? Why, then, advertisers need only one agency to co-ordinate the worldwide offensive. The Saatchi brothers set out to be that agency. But first they needed to have the critical mass to match the size of the largest advertisers. With voracious appetite, they began gobbling up firms around the globe. Their biggest acquisition was Ted Bates Advertising. In 1986, they paid a whopping $450 million for the New York giant, an unheard-of sum for an advertising agency.

The year before, the Saatchis made their first foray into Canada, a minor player on the world advertising stage, but nonetheless considered strategically important as a gateway into the vast U.S. market. The brothers bought Hayhurst Advertising, a venerable mid-sized Toronto agency founded in 1928 by Frederick Hedley Hayhurst.

"I don't think it'll make much difference to the Canadian ad business if only two of the top 10 (agencies) are Canadian," commented company scion Jim Hayhurst in an interview with *Marketing* after the sale went through.

"I suppose there is the spectre of decisions in New York affecting the business here, both in terms of profit demand and the way that employees are treated. But we've moved away from the way agencies were run in Canada during the 1950s and '60s, when one principal owned the business anyway.

"People won't be treated again like they were back then. Businesses are being run more and more by hired guns, and I suppose people will be treated more distantly than they were in the past.

"I suppose those things considered, I have a sense of regret at having sold Hayhurst. But there is no way we could have grown ourselves. In terms of the long-range servicing of our clients there is no regret at all. It was absolutely the right decision. The right business decision."

So fell Hayhurst Advertising, and with it one of the pillars of Canadian advertising. The "old grey lady," as the agency was affectionately known, had become just another cipher in the Saatchi global equation.

Bell joined the company in 1988 as creative director, a prestigious position at the top of the agency ranks. He had been flattered to be given command of the firm's copywriters and art directors. It meant a boost in salary, executive privileges, enhanced stature and respect from his peer group. As creative director, he would be ultimately responsible for the agency's advertising output. The final arbiter of quality. The man who would rally the creative department, and become the company's public face.

But as it turned out, it also meant more meetings, bureaucratic wrangling, longer hours and less time to write ads.

He became increasingly disillusioned, to the point where he jumped at the chance to go back to writing ad copy full time. In December of 1990, he left for MacLaren:Lintas, unprepared for the commotion that was to nearly wreck his career less than two months later.

While he was at Saatchi & Saatchi, Bell worked with Bruce Philp, an account executive with the brains, looks and never-say-die attitude that mark the best "Suits."

In the advertising world, a Suit handles the business side of the agency. He is the liaison with the client—the person who presides over strategy meetings and presents the agency's ad concepts. If a client has a problem or query that needs addressing, he turns to a Suit for answers.

Suits wear suits because they are meant to mirror the client. And clients wear suits. Art directors and copywriters, on the other hand, are referred to as "Creatives," and dress accordingly. They wear jeans, have long hair (as often as not tied in ponytails) and generally look and behave like the art-school graduates many of them are.

Suits are sober and square, and Creatives are brash and trendy. It has been that way since the free-wheeling 1960s ushered in a new era of artistic expression, and it became chic for Creatives to look the part. They happily chucked their ties and grey flannel suits and embraced the clothes and demeanour, if not the proletarian polemics, of counter-culture rebels.

There was little doubt which group Philp belonged to. Natty in pinstripes and carefully coiffed and groomed, he was just the man Hayter needed to head Vickers & Benson's department of account executives. He was articulate, well mannered and ambitious. He also had a reputation for forward thinking, and had a firm grasp on the latest marketing theories.

Hayter hired Philp as senior vice-president and director of client services, making him in the process a key member of the agency's inner sanctum.

At the same time as he was beefing up his staff, Hayter was thinking about other major changes. In particular, he was concerned about the high cost of the agency's Toronto offices, a six-storey building just north of the city's busiest liquor store.

It was tastefully outfitted with a costly collection of pine furniture, antiques, Inuit sculpture and other Canadiana *objets d'art.* But the building was also a ridiculous waste of space. A dominating spiral staircase ran up the building's spine, serving nothing more than a decorative function.

The fact that different floors housed separate departments also contributed to an insularity that Hayter, Satterthwaite and the other newly arrived managers found nettlesome.

Account service and direct marketing were on the sixth floor, the creative people on the fifth, sales promotion on the fourth, accounting on the third, the media department on the second. A large reception area dominated the ground floor. The arrangement caused frequent communication problems, and certainly stood in the way of developing a cohesive, integrated team atmosphere.

The only place to meet and mingle was in "O'Malley's," the fifth-floor bar that Terry O'Malley had designed from the same plans as The Spaniard Pub in Kinsale, Ireland, home of the Irish International Advertising Festival. O'Malley had visited the festival as a judge and seminar speaker, and fell in love with the place. No expense was spared to duplicate the ambience of the Irish original. O'Malley's had a working fireplace, a darts area and nineteenth-century stand-up wooden bar.

As attractive as the offices were, there was no escaping the fact that the building had flaws. Satterthwaite was amazed to find, for example, that the entrance to the underground parking lot was heated by overhead gas jets that fired up automatically when the temperature dipped in the winter. It was a luxury that the agency could ill afford, and Satterthwaite ordered the gas shut off.

Worse than the cost, the heated driveway was also a magnet for vagrants looking to keep the chill at bay on blustery nights. Each morning they would have to be chased out, empty liquor bottles littering their trail.

After failing to persuade the landlord to renegotiate the lease, Hayter and Satterthwaite agreed the only solution was to move. They decided on a site a couple of miles due north. The offices would be designed to their exacting specifications, with a move-in date scheduled for summer 1994.

Ironically, their new neighbour would be Axmith McIntyre Wicht Ltd., formerly known as Camp Associates Advertising Ltd., the agency founded in 1959 by Progressive Conservative backroom strategist Dalton Camp, and the former home of such Tory notables as Senator Norman Atkins and Hugh Segal, who dallied with the notion of entering the 1993 leadership race to replace Brian Mulroney.

But it wouldn't be the first time Vickers & Benson would find itself cheek by jowl with a competitor of a different political stripe. Hayter climbed into bed with the Tories only five months after he joined the agency.

Looking to beef up Vickers & Benson's media operation, he began talking to Peter Simpson, a renegade adman turned movie mogul, who pioneered the concept of independent media buying in Canada in 1968. Ten years later, he founded Norstar Entertainment, a production company known for churning out low-brow but immensely popular movies.

Simpson sold his original firm, Media Buying Services, in the early 1980s. He started a similar enterprise, Media Canada, in 1984 to buy ad time and space for the new Mulroney government, which was then on the road to becoming the country's largest advertiser. By 1992, the Feds were spending more than $113 million a year on ads, millions more than such market-place heavyweights as General Motors of Canada and Procter & Gamble Inc.

Hayter and Simpson were, and remain, strange bedfellows. The one was earnest, straightforward and urbane; the other, boastful, hard-driving and plain-spoken. They were also coloured different political hues: Hayter's Grit red to Simpson's Tory blue.

Implausible though it would seem, the two men struck a deal in August 1991 to join forces. Vickers & Benson's media department would merge with Simpson's Media Canada to form Genesis Media Inc. The combined operation was instantly propelled into the top ranks of Canada's media-buying operations.

"There is an urgent need for Canadian agencies to respond to the rapidly changing media environment in this country," Hayter said as the deal was announced. "The pressure to provide more media value for our clients has never been more urgent and meeting these demands is a top V&B priority.

"We want to work in concert with the media to innovate and add value for the benefit of our clients."

Added Simpson: "I have known John for more than twenty years. We share a common vision of how the world of media planning, creativity, buying and innovation is evolving, and I totally share John's commitment and enthusiasm about Genesis."

Publicly, neither Hayter nor Simpson said their differing politics should get in the way of a good business deal. "We don't see the political differences as a negative," Simpson said.

Privately, Hayter was not so sure. He still gets nervous talking about working for the Liberals, as he did during the last federal election, while a company under his partnership control was buying media for the then Conservative government. It required a deft balancing act that only someone with Hayter's marketing moxie could hope to achieve, or dare to try.

With the office move planned, the Genesis deal signed, and with Jim Satterthwaite, Terry Bell and Bruce Philp on board, Hayter was ready to lead a new-look management team charged with whipping Vickers & Benson back into fighting trim.

Three other men, all members of the agency's old guard, were also part of the team: O'Malley, who with Bremner gone, was one of the agency's last remaining links with its fabled past; Joe Warwick, O'Malley's long-time cohort; and the irascible Mike McCormick, who presided over the firm's direct-marketing arm.

Together this trio represented the Vickers & Benson that had been; Satterthwaite, Bell and Philp represented the Vickers & Benson that was yet to be.

And orchestrating the lot was Hayter, who sought harmony from the discord.

# CHAPTER 2

H AYTER KNEW Vickers & Benson was in trouble. Not that there was risk of imminent collapse. Far from it. As Canada's thirteenth biggest ad firm with annual gross revenues of $15 million, the agency still commanded incontestable clout.

Yet he was anxious. The omens were everywhere and, after thirty years on both sides of the ad fence, Hayter had developed a knack for divining warning signs.

If there was one thing he had learned, it was the ability to spot a marketing crisis in the making. And as long as Vickers & Benson stayed its present course the company was headed for a fall. Big time. It wouldn't happen in a day or even a year. But his innate disaster detector told him the clock was ticking, that the slow rot had set in.

The agency had lost its edge in a business where image and momentum are valued above all else. Age and tradition had dulled the killer instinct, the drive to best all comers. The staff were rootless, insecure, lacking in motivation and hungry for leadership. Little new business, the lifeblood of any agency, had come knocking, and the buzz on the street said existing clients were ripe for the plucking.

McDonald's Restaurants, one of Vickers & Benson's cornerstone accounts, was preparing to shift its multi-million-dollar national account. Compounding the problem, the Ontario Liberals, a party the agency helped put into office, were trounced at the polls by the New Democrats under Bob Rae.

Vickers & Benson had already suffered when the federal Liberals lost in 1984. As a true Grit agency, that meant the loss of lucrative contacts and contracts. History was repeated when David Peterson was shot down, and the province's big-budget tourism account skidded out the door.

While he was mulling over his next move, Hayter received a lengthy memo from Bob Topping, the agency's former director of client services and an old-guard member of eighteen years' standing.

It was an impassioned, lay-it-on-the-line missive designed to provoke and challenge.

"V&B has an incredible ability of holding onto people's hearts long after they have left the company," Topping began. "I think you have a big job in figuring out what it is that causes this phenomenon and keeping it alive. It's what brings people to V&B, keeps them here and keeps them loving the place even when some of them are working at the competition.

"I fear we could lose some of that now. We've lost many of the key people that kept it alive before and we seem to be approaching business like many of the big international agencies. That is not V&B and we could lose some of the character that makes us unique... Family cannot be thought of as a bad concept, and arrogance will never be its replacement."

He was equally frank about the feud simmering in the ranks:

"I feel like we are in a stage where there is too much energy spent figuring out what is wrong with V&B and our people. I suppose that is a natural process when many new people come into a company, but it could become a very destructive influence while the many pieces are being put back together. I think it is too easy to pigeonhole people based on what they appear to be at this precise moment. It is a much more difficult job to see what people can become with the proper direction, training and patience. You know I have been somewhat protective of a few people recently and I think it would be wrong to classify it as over-protective. It takes all kinds of people to run a large company, particularly one with the range of clients of V&B. Everybody cannot fit one mold and it would be a tragedy if the 'I'd clear the entire department out if I could' mentality actually took hold.

"Clear out the true deadwood, go get a few superstars and then work with these people and give them a chance. Some of them may not 'get it,' but they sure are hard-working and loyal and for the most part, smart and capable enough if applied in the right place."

Topping then offered a timely warning:

"I think V&B is on a cultural collision course with itself. We don't know what we are right now. We have a collection of capable people each working in their own areas, but there is not the synergy that is needed. I find that most of your managers have a strong one-on-one relationship with you, John, but the group is not functioning anything like the team it should. I think this is the next stage for the management group but it won't come from a few meetings a year. It has to be a more natural process for senior management to work together on a regular basis.

"I think you should take a core group into the inner track with you, Jim and Terry and let them be part of the creation of the next V&B. The final version of the V&B Vision should come from this group so that they can all feel that part of it belongs to them."

Topping, once the senior manager on the McDonald's account, urged Hayter to take a leaf from the chain's management stylebook:

"I have been particularly impressed with McDonald's over the years. Somehow this enormous company with thousands of shareholders has created an environment in which a group of officers act like they own the company themselves. If there is an issue within their company they pull whatever group of officers is available and together they deal with the issue.

"Somehow we have never really captured this approach and it would seem very simple if we wanted to create it. The power of partnership and participation is incredible when applied."

Next, some thoughts on restructuring:

"It is essential for the company to come to terms with its evolving two sides. On one side is the new group with a goal of creating a higher level of strategic and creative work, particularly in the advertising area. On the other side is, for the most part, the older guard who deal at a different level but who have been very successful at managing accounts that appreciate their (and the V&B) approach. There is in my opinion a big risk of this second group becoming a second class of citizen with V&B, and they should not be.

"These two cultures can exist with one another but only if each tries to understand and appreciate the other. In fact, V&B needs both. We need to raise our creative product to a higher level without question, but this alone will not win accounts like Canada's Wonderland [a Toronto theme park whose account Vickers & Benson handled in the early 1980s]. We lost Wonderland years ago for the same reason. Gary Gray [a former creative director] and his team created the most wonderful image commercials you could imagine for the park, but they couldn't understand the needs of Wonderland the retailer."

Topping, an avowed O'Malley loyalist, ended with a plea that Hayter find an appropriate role for his long-time boss:

"In my opinion he is the finest single asset this company has ever had. Terry's role has changed, probably for all the right reasons but his role has to be redefined. You need to determine a way to apply this incredible person to the business of the future in a way that allows Terry to flourish."

One final admonition:

"John, you have an enormous task ahead of you. You are the caretaker of this wonderful creature that is V&B. There are some amazing qualities to V&B and yet it has needed so many changes in order to keep it alive and healthy into the next generation of V&Bers. You are only part way through the process and it is a difficult one with many opinions on all sides on how how you should do it."

Hayter had other worries besides the internal hurdles. Of equal concern was the fact that advertisers were changing, putting fresh demands not only on his firm but every agency, large and small. Slick TV commercials were no longer a panacea; advertisers wanted smarter, gutsier solutions.

As a group, they were pouring more and more dollars into "below-the-line marketing"—industry shorthand meaning promotions, contests, coupons, direct mail, PR, joint programs with allied firms and any other gambit that might make cash registers ring in a market-place soured by recession.

Who had time for expensive image-building campaigns that might take months, or years, to generate results? Forget the three-martini lunches and costly commercial shoots on exotic Caribbean islands.

Schmoozing and padded expense accounts were things of the past. No one could afford the gilded lifestyle of the go-for-it eighties in a decade of buttoned-down austerity.

Marketing departments were being slashed, and ad budgets squeezed like sponges. Every promotional dollar had to work harder, and be put to better use, than ever before.

More than the lousy economy was responsible for the ennui. Consumers were also changing. They could no longer be hoodwinked by glib pitches promising whiter this and brighter that.

Their sales resistance grew despite all the advances marketers had made in the science of persuasion. Consumers were dissected by demographics (their age, income and professions), and defined by psychographics (their attitudes and values towards a product or company). Sociologists had been deployed to untangle the complexities of ethnic populations, of women, of gays, of virtually any subgroup considered to be prospects.

Focus groups, random sampling, people meters to measure audience ratings, pre- and post-campaign testing—all had become standard operating procedure by the wired-in nineties.

To little avail. Not only were they harder to reach, consumers had also become jaded after too many hyped-up promises of product performance. They no longer believed nationally advertised brands were always worth their premium price-stickers. Private-label products marketed by retailers, like the President's Choice line sold by the Loblaw's supermarket chain, were seen to offer comparable quality at often significant savings.

The erosion of consumer confidence and brand loyalty sent shockwaves through the marketing community. In their quest for a magic bullet, companies turned to self-proclaimed gurus flogging concepts like

Total Quality Management and Continuous Improvement. Empowerment begat paradigm shifts begat self-organizing systems.

One hot button after another was pushed in a frantic search for a cure-all. Marketers dallied with in-store radio networks, video monitors in shopping malls, ads over urinals. Blimps with electronic signs flew high over cities, while automated telemarketing computers made in-home sales calls. Direct marketers flooded the postal system with junk mail, and advertisers paid handsomely for movie producers to plug their wares on the silver screen.

Advertisers even tried to titillate consumers from their lethargy. The Benetton clothing chain used billboards featuring androgynous body parts stamped—or were they tatooed for identification?—with the phrase "HIV positive." What did AIDS have to do with designer sweaters? Nobody cared.

Naked models hawked Calvin Klein's pricey perfumes in sexy magazine ads, while rapper Marky Mark grabbed his crotch in TV commercials for underwear. Consumers yawned.

There was no quick fix, no easing of the sales slide. By 1993, advertisers were desperate for a whipping boy. They had to look no further than their agencies.

Hugo Powell, president of Labatt Breweries, struck a sympathetic chord in a blistering speech delivered to an advertising congress in Toronto in January that year.

He lashed out at agencies for being out of step, for failing to acknowledge that clients were seeking new communications answers in a time of crisis. Too many agencies, he charged, were peopled with sycophantic "handlers" and middle-management meddlers whose only purpose was to perpetuate an outmoded system no one could afford.

Other advertisers soon swelled the chorus of detractors. Ian

McIntosh, the general manager of consumer products at Goodyear Canada, complained to anyone within earshot that too many agencies pushed superfluous services at exhorbitant costs.

The tire and tune-up chain fired its big multinational agency and hired a small start-up firm promising senior talent and none of the frills.

"I think clients are tired of paying the freight for a lot of overhead," McIntosh lamented to the trade journal *Strategy*. "I'm not singling out multinational agencies, but I am taking a shot at the process itself. Advertising agencies need to go back to doing what they do best, and that is advertising.... We don't need all the extra bodies and offices and layers of departments."

The condemnations were not confined to Canada. The rhetoric was even more savage in the U.S. Each week the American trade magazines were filled with hand-wringing articles about the calamities wrenching the business. Even *Fortune* magazine joined the fray in a critique tauntingly titled: "Do You Need Your Ad Agency?"

Viewers "are zapping ads even as the media marketplace gets more turbulent by the day," noted author Patricia Sellers. "Brand equity, that commercial karma between consumers and products, is eroding universally. As a result, connecting with consumers today requires more ads more often—but without more cost—produced and delivered in new, unusual ways.

"Yet the agencies have been devising big, expensive, cookie-cutter campaigns for these increasingly fickle audiences in much the same way that top-heavy, vertically integrated, multilayered manufacturers used to produce automobiles no one would buy—and at cost plus 15% commission, no less. Now, just like manufacturing, the advertising industry is undergoing seismic change."

The message had been resoundingly heard. Agencies scurried to "reengineer" (their euphemism for lay-offs), pushing unemployment in the ad sector to new peaks. Recession had already decimated the agency workforce, forcing survivors to shoulder more and heavier loads. The new cost-cutting frenzy only added to their burden.

The lesson was painfully clear: Get lean or lose big. No agency, no matter how large, could afford the escalating overhead at a time when advertisers were paring spending to the bone.

The turmoil took its toll on the bottom line. The Institute of Canadian Advertising, the agencies' trade association, reported that industry profits had free-fallen by half.

"Agencies do not command the client respect that they did ten or twenty years ago," warned ICA president John Sinclair. "No longer are they considered a marketing partner, but simply a supplier. This lack of credibility demands that agencies do a better job of being accountable and really demonstrating the value of what they do.

"It also demands that agencies understand the real problems of their clients and not be seen as purveyors only of media advertising. They must be prepared to concentrate on short-term advertising results, not just building a brand-image over the long haul."

Any agency that didn't recognize that, that failed to make substantive changes, was just moving deckchairs around on the Titanic.

Like just about everyone else in the ad business, Sinclair had his own opinions about the ailing industry. The crisis, he believed, was really an opportunity in disguise, one that agencies could exploit if they hunkered down and made the necessary adjustments.

In a speech to the Advertising Agencies Association of British Columbia, Sinclair preached his theory in the form of Ten Commandments:

1. Thou shalt be full-service.

Be super-duper, all-in, ultra-wide full service. Offer direct marketing, public relations, sales promotion, database marketing, event marketing, sponsorships. The works. Because if you don't, two things happen. The door is open for another marketing supplier to start wooing your client and, more importantly, your client may get the feeling that you're a media advertising specialist with limited marketing perspectives.

2. Thou shalt be integrated.

It is critically important that all your marketing services be developed in a fully integrated and seamless manner and that they all speak with one voice, from one strategy. If the collateral services appear to be add-ons, or the client is told that George from your promotion arm or Susan from your PR module will be out to see them next week, watch out. Your client will soon begin to wonder if he should be dealing with George and Susan, or whether they really are tuned into the mainline advertising strategy.

3. Thou shalt address short-term advertising goals.

Yes, it's important to build a company or brand image, which may take time. But no longer can you say to your client: "Give me a million dollars a year and in three years' time you'll have a strong image out there." He's worried about this year, or this quarter, or sometimes this month. He may be out of a job next year or the company may be out of business next year. Today, it is essential to talk short-term advertising results.

4. Thou shalt know your operating costs.

Sounds pretty basic, but I'm referring to pricing the services you sell to clients. You must know your real costs of developing promotions or creating a new television commercial or providing strategic counsel. You must be able to price your product fairly and competitively.

Gone are the days of straight 15 per cent commission. The commission system fouled up the whole industry, because it provided high revenues oftentimes, and thereby permitted the agency to give away other services. Those giveaways are no longer okay, because the high commissions have disappeared.

5. Thou shalt develop an agency personality.

Find a niche, develop a difference, break out of the pack. I'm appalled at clients who tell me that, after listening to three or four new-business presentations in a single day, they sometimes have trouble recollecting which agency was which. The agencies all say about the same thing about themselves, in the same manner and leave the impression that basically they all are the same. I recognize that to develop a unique agency personality is easier said than done, but it can be accomplished.

6. Thou shalt be selective in new business pursuits.

Don't chase every prospect and certainly don't produce [speculative] creative on request. Choose six or eight prospects you'd like and concentrate on them. Start with a letter, force a conversation or a lunch, be patient and be persistent. Expect to be courting them for years. Don't give up. And when you're asked to prepare spec creative, ask to be well paid for it.

7. Thou shalt run a financially tight ship.

Be vigilant about your expenses. Be very careful about the creditworthiness of your clients. ICA believes that the agency should act as the principal of all media transactions, but if client credit comes into question, make sure you write a risk-free contract to cover yourself. One bad debt of any size can undermine the financial stability of any agency.

8. Thou shalt be accountable.

Clients nowadays expect a proven return for their advertising investments, and they deserve it. They get it on trade promotions and they get it on direct marketing. They expect and deserve a measurable payback on advertising. Be prepared to support your recommendations, with pre-test research or case histories, if necessary. Be prepared to show how advertising has paid out for similar companies and similar advertising budgets.

9. Thou shalt concentrate on creative excellence.

This is the backbone of our business. It is impossible to look elsewhere and get the same calibre of creative work that the good agencies offer. Hire the best creatives you can find and pay them well and keep them happy. They will reward you by doing good work, going up fewer blind alleys and they will help put your agency on the map. It is unlikely that you can build a hot agency on the basis of your media or promotions department. Brilliant creative will make up for all kinds of other shortcomings of an agency.

10. Thou shalt streamline thy agency structure.

Many people think agencies are already streamlined. Here's what Tom Peters says in his latest book, *Liberation Management:* "We tend to think of ad agencies as zippy. Yet many mature ad firms have developed the same symptoms of advanced bureaucracy— grotesque overspecialization, wars between the tribes (the creative side, account executives), title-itis, and so on—that mark dying industrial outfits." The structure of your agencies should be re-invented.

Think through a zero-based organizational structure. Would you build it the same if you started your business all over again? Look for new ways to streamline your agency people structure. If this streamlining process is done diligently, it will assist you in pricing your

services more competitively, giving better value to your clients—
something your client needs and expects these days.

While Hayter ruminated on the fragile state of his industry and what it
portended for Vickers & Benson, other agency executives were already
mobilizing.

Ron Telpner, a senior officer with McKim Baker Lovick/BBDO, Canada's
largest ad firm, was among those convinced that mainstream agencies
like his were dinosaurs too big and ponderous to adapt to new realities.

He quit the agency to set up his own Toronto-based shop called The
Brainstorm Group, with the mandate to offer advertisers a spectrum of
marketing and communications options. The goal was to provide top-
level thinking without the usual agency mark-ups and bureaucratic
bumbling.

It was a model borrowed from Tony Long, a Toronto adman who
formed his own consultancy in 1978 as an alternative to the "establishment" agencies. With a core group of on-staff experts and a wide circle
of freelancers, he set out to show that advertisers could get comparable
service, and save money to boot.

At first, many in the ad community scoffed. But Long proved prescient
in one key area—integrated marketing at à la carte prices grew to be an
unstoppable force.

Telpner was itching to join the bandwagon. "The Brainstorm Group is
truly an agency of the 1990s," he said in announcing his new enterprise.
"We'll work directly with clients or through their agency to bring
inspired, integrated thinking through creative people. Not handlers."

On the day Telpner hung out his Brainstorm shingle, an outfit with an
even tighter focus was formed by two young Toronto admen who also
despaired of the big agency scene.

Art director Duncan Bruce and copywriter Brad Myers promised their new partnership, Bruce & Myers Creative Directions Inc., would challenge conventional wisdom.

"The advertising industry is undergoing a paradigm shift," said Myers. "Globally, innovative agencies are reorganizing by discipline into 'pods' [agencyspeak for small work units]. Such groupings appear to be the future. Working our own way, in a creative pod, with clients who want what we offer, we hope to play an important role in Canadian advertising."

"We're not an agency, and won't become one," added Bruce. "We're creative entrepreneurs, who want to own something. We don't work on commission. We don't give speculative presentations. We sell our minds, and work only on contract."

Others explored different routes. Brad Robins and Bill Sharpe, respectively the chairman and president of Robins Sharpe Associates Ltd., agreed their agency's future lay with the Toronto office of DDB Needham Worldwide, a unit of the giant New York-based Omnicom Group. They sold their mid-sized firm in the summer of 1993.

What attracted them was DDB Needham's decision to institute a new way of creating ads. Instead of a hierarchical structure, there would be a system of "service clusters" (yet another buzzword for business units) with the amoebic ability to split and reform as client dictates demanded.

"This is not a traditional merger," DDB Needham president and chief executive Paul Carder insisted. "Robins Sharpe will operate independently, but where appropriate they will draw on the broader resources of DDB Needham, domestically and internationally."

In turn, DDB Needham would draw on the creative resources of Robins Sharpe as needed. This was positioned as one of those "synergistic opportunities" marketing folk are so prone to prattle on about.

The cluster concept is the brainchild of Keith Reinhard, DDB Needham's New York chairman.

"Do we integrate? When it fits a client's need," he told *Advertising Age*. "The old one-size-fits-all is gone. One client may say, 'All I want is great film [commercials].' But if he comes up with a new product and wants to talk about where he ought to go with that product, then what does the cluster do? It changes into a marketing group."

Reinhard is convinced this is the future of the agency business.

"There's a difference between an entrepreneurial thinker and a traditional thinker," he said. "We're looking for the people who reject the idea of being a follower. In the old system, people were motivated by authority. In the new system, the real god is the idea."

Reinhard was not the only one to pounce on the power of the idea. Sitting in his spartan corner office overlooking bustling Yonge Street on a warm May morning in 1993, Hayter was thinking along a parallel line.

Ideas—or more specifically, big creative ideas—are what advertisers need most from agencies. Everything else—the ads, the choice of media, servicing the account—is merely execution. But the process must start with an idea that is so clever, so breakthrough, so unexpected, that advertisers will demand to see it put into action.

Hayter had little doubt that Vickers & Benson's salvation lay in its ability to consistently generate ideas. Not just competent ones, but the best in the market.

Of course, any adman will tell you he wants to create ads built on "big ideas" that set his clients apart from the pack. Hayter wanted the commitment to be more than lip service. He wanted "big ideas" to be an integral part of every campaign and in every discipline.

Vickers & Benson already had some success in this area, but the record was spotty.

Hayter was especially pleased with campaigns developed for Bank of Montreal, Amstel beer and Gatorade.

In fact, he felt the bank's "We're Paying Attention" ads were outflanking the competition. Through a series of TV commercials, the message of a caring, responsive bank was emerging. Vignettes and testimonials were used to great effect. There was senior citizen Mrs. McIlquham, who appreciated the attention she got from her local branch. "I think your bank manager is tops," she says at the end of the commercial, her voice cracking.

Then there was the spot about the cabbie, crabbing about the traffic congestion and frantic pace of city life. His only satisfaction was that he was saving Air Miles for a dream vacation, courtesy of Bank of Montreal.

The campaign for Amstel was also being recognized as an innovative breath of fresh air in a category where every beer commercial seemed indistinguishable from the next.

The Amstel ads shunned stereotypic and sexist images of leggy blondes in tight halter tops to celebrate the individuality and integrity of "real" people, and the taste and quality of the beer itself.

One commercial shows a stressed-out boomer twirling his answering machine by the cord and letting it fly through the air. Another has a group of friends in a bar crowding around a bashful man. "We have one for Gary Round, who said 'no' to the transfer because he likes where he is already," the announcer intones. Another simply shows a bottle of Amstel sliding down the length of a bar. "It's not complicated," the announcer says. "It's not trendoid. It's got character. Ummm. Character. What a novel idea! Amstel. We have one for you."

The message was driven home in print ads. One award-winning

version showed a condom, an Amstel beer cap and a single line of copy: "Because you didn't wait for her to mention it." The ad tacitly trumpets Amstel drinkers for knowing that practising safe sex is the responsible thing to do.

The Gatorade campaign also made the product—and by extension, those who drank it—the hero. A series of transit-shelter posters showed sweaty, macho types swigging back their favourite thirst quencher. "Separates the Men from the Water Boys," the headline bragged. The implication: Designer water is for wimps; real athletes drink Gatorade.

Each of the campaigns were built around "big ideas," not one-offs with short-term appeal. Each created a personality—and a leadership position—for the advertiser. Hayter wanted the same for every client. And he wanted it extended across every medium. That was not always the case even for Bank of Montreal, Amstel and Gatorade. Sometimes there was a tie-in between the ads and, say, the public-relations or sales-promotion components. But even that was inconsistent.

Hayter would only be happy when the same idea was integrated through every discipline, every time. But how to get there? How could he get the others in the agency, especially the old guard, to buy into his plan?

Hayter held no illusions about how difficult that would be. But at least he had a goal. And he also had the mission statement he wrote six months earlier to guide him.

The seven-page manifesto is written from two perspectives. The first part presented an idealized picture of Vickers & Benson as seen by outsiders; the second, how a V&Ber should feel about his company and what it stands for.

Granted, it was written in highfalutin tones and read too much like a corporate Desiderata. But it was a start.

"Be known as Canada's creative powerhouse," it begins. "A constantly thinking company that provides our clients with superior thinking that delivers outstanding work, client servicing and business results."

There is more:

"Clients are proud to be with us. They trust our instincts. They respect our work ethic and our relentless pursuit to provide them with a competitive edge. They know our deep passion to be the most creative we can be covers every facet of communications from advertising to media, sales promotion, direct marketing, to client service and beyond.

"They know we strive to employ the best. They see us as an efficient, exceptionally well-managed company providing them with indisputable value. They know we are profitable and solid. They understand this profitability funds our never-ending commitment to be the best we can be.

"They like us because we are open. Honest. Humane. Co-operative. And work in and for our community. V&B is the place where our competitors would like to be. It has a respectful and sensitive working environment. Prospects contemplating an agency change consistently have us at the top of their selection list. Some even choose us without a competition. When we are on a list, we are the feared opponent. The one the others wonder what we will do. We are what other agencies would like to be and can't. Because we offer greater opportunity."

The next section reworks the theme from a personal point of view:

"We have the best front-line talent and the best bench in the industry. We have re-defined the process of how to get great work done. We feel positive, productive and efficient. There's minimal waste and duplication. Because of these traits, we are a team and enjoy working together. We have fun and we show it. We can accept constructive criticism and will not allow ego to prevail over what is right.

"Our successes are shared and that keeps us close, informed, trusting and respectful of one another. We are truly passionate about the work. We understand and revel in competition. This translates into the need to be constantly pushing for the most within each of us. We can make the tough decisions in a professional and compassionate way. We always give the extra effort because we desperately want to win.

"When the job is done, we know we must relax and get away from it all. To recharge, refresh and renew. And we do it. We are clearly the best in our business at uncovering highly leverable strategies. This allows us to unleash our creative minds with full freedom and strength to take clear aim at our clients' best business opportunities. We do this better than anyone. And we do it across all communication fronts because we are confident we have equal capability in each discipline. This is enhanced because we know we are the most experienced in recognizing when we can multiply our clients' dollars through a varied but integrated communications attack."

And still more:

"As long as they help our clients achieve their goals, we believe in and seek meaningful industry awards which publicly recognize our work as being creatively superior. Without arrogance or cockiness, we enjoy being profiled and talked about.

"We have mastered what our competitors haven't. That's how to best apply our resources of time and technology within our streamlined workflow process which moves our work from start to finish with minimal waste. Our efficiency translates to fewer people doing more and better work faster. This delivers superior margins. As a result, we are able to appropriately compensate all our people. Our best and brightest are compensated at levels not achievable elsewhere. They share in our successes and in our growth.

"We are proud to be Canadian. We are V&Bers."

Long on philosophy but short on practicality, the mission statement detailed where the agency should be, but not how to get there.

So in the best tradition of Vickers & Benson, Hayter called his management team together to try to chart a path to this Holy Grail. There was no time for rhetoric and platitudes. What was needed now was a blueprint.

# CHAPTER 3

T HEY WERE A disparate lot. Save for their sex (male), race (white) and age (hovering in middle age), their appearances held little else in common.

Sitting at the head of the antique pine table in the sixth-floor conference room was Hayter, a football player in his youth and still a bulldog of a man in his early fifties. Longish hair now thinning, he was nattily dressed in white shirt, floral tie and black loafers.

On his right was second-in-command Jim Satterthwaite, sitting sideways, his legs stretched out on the chair beside him. A tall man, English by birth but North American by temperament, he had a greying beard and wore a white dress shirt with a tie striped red and blue. With disconcerting effect, he peered over his half-moon glasses—his left eye brown, the right blue.

At the other end of the table sat account head Bruce Philp. Still in his mid-thirties, he was the youngest in the room, a Woodstock-generation kid who long ago traded in his bell bottoms for a flashy Bay Street suit.

Styled hair, trimmed beard. His suit jacket was slung carefully across his chair back.

His neighbour was fortysomething director of creative services Terry Bell, casually attired in open-neck striped shirt over a white T-shirt; faded jeans, white socks and loafers. His steely white hair and beard contrasted sharply with his jet-black reading glasses.

Next to him was direct-marketing chief Mike McCormick, a scowling ex-Montrealer in his late forties with a potbelly and a penchant for gaudy ties. Like Bell, he was in jeans and loafers. The sleeves on his rumpled shirt were rolled, his glasses perched on top of his head.

And sitting on Hayter's left was O'Malley, the company patriarch. His wavy hair was salt and pepper, but the rakish moustache belied his fifty-six years. He was wearing an immaculate white shirt and an elegant silk tie. A veteran runner and *habitué* of the YMCA, he had the physique of a man half his age.

Perhaps it was the spring sun's lazy languor. Or maybe there had been just too many late meetings and early deadlines. Whatever the reasons, the men gathered around the table seemed distracted, detached. Bell stared out the window, eyes blank and unfocused. O'Malley fiddled with an elastic band. McCormick yawned.

All this navel-gazing was making them listless. Hayter had already led them through two previous meetings to try to figure a way to kick-start the agency. They had agreed Vickers & Benson should become a "creative powerhouse," but each had differing views on how to do it. The encounters had been gruelling. Tempers flared. Turf wars exploded.

Now they were being forced to endure yet another brainstorming session. Would this one be any more productive? They were startled from their private reveries as Hayter started to speak.

"We have been really hard on ourselves," he began, recapping the progress to date. "We have been very critical. We went through each of our communications skills from advertising to what we call 'promotion advertising,' sales promotion to direct marketing to public relations. Even our studio. And we took a look at our media division very quickly. We listed all the conditions to be a powerhouse in each of those areas.

"In almost every case, the list of where we were missing was very long."

In the earlier meetings, much time had been spent debating a brutal review their own staff had given them. Their words were harsh and unsparing. There was no leadership, they complained. No vision and too much rhetoric.

"The feedback we got from our people was certainly enlightening, and not necessarily surprising," Hayter reminded his colleagues. "But when you ask somebody to come in and give you a report card, and they hit you kind of hard and frequently and very critically, it certainly gets your attention."

So what to do about getting Vickers & Benson back on track? The answer, Hayter said, had to be developing more "big ideas" for clients. But to do that, each department would first have to sharpen its skills, to become a "centre of excellence." Otherwise the idea, no matter how big or small, would languish on the drawing board.

And instead of each unit working independently and, as was currently too often the case, at cross purposes, there would have to be much greater interdepartmental co-operation to carry the big idea through each stage of development.

The goal, Hayter summarized, "is to be the company that delivers the ideas that allow every client to differentiate itself from the competition. In other words, our ideas are so powerful that they give our clients a

competitive advantage over anyone else. And then we have these centres of excellence that drive it in every direction."

But how to become a "big ideas" company?

In the previous meeting, Hayter had blue-skyed a possibility. Why not
establish a core group of strategists to invent the ideas? Sort of a central
brain trust whose only responsibility would be to invent brilliant solutions.

But not everyone had bought into the concept, and even those who
had disagreed over how the agency could make the scheme workable.

"At the end of the meeting we were all sort of drained and felt we
needed to think privately, and I know we all have done that," Hayter
continued. "Mike suggested that maybe the best way to really maximize
the potential in the direct-marketing division is to have his account
managers report to Bruce Philp, who's in charge of account management for the advertising department.

"In other words, account management goes into one person. We still
have creative people who are specialists in direct marketing, but the
strategy and client contact is developed by a single core group. That
sort of stimulated this 'big idea' invention group.

"The thing that intrigues me about that is that in any organization
there are a handful of people able to develop the big ideas. Whether
you're a multinational agency or a Vickers & Benson, there's a core
group that does it. I know Young & Rubicam, when I was there, had two
or three people they'd send all over the world. If there was a problem
they'd send them, because they were the best.

"Now if we had such a core group shouldn't they be working on every
client's business? Then we have those people who are terrific at execut-
ing the ideas. And that's where we left off."

As Hayter ended his recap, Philp handed out photocopies of two articles he felt provided clues on how the agency might be repositioned. Both were from the Autumn 1990 edition of *Business Quarterly,* published by the University of Western Ontario in London.

The first, "Prescription for the '90s: The Boundary-less Company," was written by William Blundell, who had then just retired as chairman and chief executive officer of General Electric Canada Inc. The second, "The Employee Empowerment Era," was by business professor Jeffrey Gandz.

Blundell's article chronicled the challenges facing Canadian companies.

"During the '80s," he wrote, "many of us charted our course using three key ingredients—reality, openness and ownership. One important change in leadership style that evolved during that period was the transition from the notion of 'managing' to the notion of 'leading,' that is, a change to less measuring and controlling, and more emphasis on vision and open communication to the complete workforce. Our transformation in the '80s was largely confined to upper management. In the 1990s, it will involve enlisting the support of every person in the company."

Blundell argued that companies must focus harder on their customers, allow their employees to make more decisions and break down the walls that stifle innovation.

"We in management need to shift gears once again as we did from the controls and management of earlier decades, to the restructuring of the '80s, towards a true revolution in the way we work in the '90s," he concluded.

"As competition becomes increasingly global, the reach for Canadian-based competitive edge needs to be focused on flexibility rather than scale. Flexibility can be developed and sustained by moving towards the boundary-less company; it is therefore the overpowering priority for all Canadian managers."

Gandz's article picked up the theme.

"The 1990s," he opined, "will be known as the empowerment era, the age when successful businesses finally take the steps necessary to reintegrate thinking and doing, thereby liberating the creative and innovative energies of employees to compete effectively in a global environment."

Gandz listed six essential conditions that must be met for true empowerment to take hold. Staff must be properly trained. There also has be a corporate vision all can believe in, along with a set of shared values. Benefits need to be shared, managers must trust their employees to make decisions, and they must not be afraid to take risks.

Philp took his colleagues through the articles, commenting briefly on salient points. The others around the conference table listened, but out of obligation. They didn't share Philp's love of corporate technospeak, the buzzwords and pat phrases of marketing gurus and tenured academics.

Just get on with it, their expressions said. This is boring.

Reading their impatience, Philp hastily wrapped up his spiel. There was a pause, and then Hayter began talking about a book review he had read the previous weekend. It compared the traditional way of doing business with the new thinking gaining favour in certain corporate circles.

In the old days, Hayter said, everyone in a company had very separate roles, like a baseball team. Seldom did players share positions or functions. Individual performances were all that mattered.

Then companies evolved into a structure like a soccer team, with players having multiple roles. They had to play both defence and offence, learning to pass the ball in perfect synchronicity.

But the new paradigm mimics a jazz group with everyone playing and contributing at the same time.

Hayter stood up and walked to an easel on the other side of the room. He took a marker and drew five interlocking circles.

"There could be five of us and we all play the trumpet," he said. "There could be five of us, but we overlap. But most of the skill we're bringing is unique to the group, and the combination of this is not additional. It becomes a great multiple."

The new approach does away with titles and other features of the traditional corporate hierarchy, he said. Team spirit and co-operation are paramount.

Hayter returned to his seat, the others nodding with interest. This meeting was finally going somewhere.

Picking up his thread, Hayter brought the lesson home by uttering one word—"Cossette"—a name guaranteed to grab attention. The mere mention of V&B's arch-rival was enough to elicit groans of grudging respect from the men gathered about the table.

Cossette was another large Canadian-owned agency, founded in Quebec City in 1972. Over the next twenty years it grew dramatically, setting up satellite offices in Montreal, Toronto and Vancouver. It was the Toronto office that wrested away McDonald's in 1991.

Vickers & Benson hung on to the chain's Ontario promotional assignment, but it did not have the prestige of the national account, which the agency had handled for more than a decade. The loss was a biting blow to Vickers & Benson, second only to the calamity of losing Ford in 1987. The agency had worked around the clock to save the business after McDonald's called the review. When the verdict came, tears flowed freely.

In addition to Cossette, the Toronto offices of two U.S.-based agencies, Leo Burnett and McCann-Erickson Advertising, had made presentations.

The race was "very close," Gary Reinblatt, McDonald's senior vice-president and national director of marketing, said after the contest was decided. "We felt the passion they [Cossette] had for the McDonald's account, the spirit, the teamwork, the creative effort and excellent credentials won it for them."

Though devastated, Hayter was gentlemanly in the face of defeat. The team assigned to save the business had done an outstanding job. There was nothing different he could have, or should have, done to keep McDonald's in the fold.

"When you are an incumbent, you don't start out in first place," he said at the time, referring to the slim odds of keeping an account once a client has decided to shop around.

"We went into the meeting to win, and we set the crossbar high. We didn't think anyone could jump over it—but hats off to Cossette, they did."

Eighteen months later, the loss still stung. Hayter and his companions had resolved to win the entire account back, knowing that to do so meant beating their nemesis in yet another showdown.

"The reason Cossette is successful is, I think, they're probably more focused than most Canadian agencies, whether they're Canadian-owned or not," Hayter said. "And their team has been together for a long time. They know what to expect of the other guy. When they go into a room, they know what that other guy's going to do.

"I don't think their organization is superior to what we'll have. I just think the length of time they've been together, and the fact they have formed a team camaraderie, makes them effective. So I think if you can combine the organizational structure of the future and create the camaraderie, trust and drive that a team can bring through talent, respect and all those things, it could be a pretty powerful force."

At this point, Bell, who had yet to volunteer a word, broke his silence.

"I'm confused," he said. "For going on an hour. Where is this going to?"

Philp, who was enjoying the cerebral workout, shot him an isn't-it-obvious? look. We're trying to define the ideal agency, he said.

Bell was still flustered. The group had already talked about that in previous meetings. Everyone knew what the main problems were.

"I would have thought," he said carefully, "the next step would have been to look at those things in terms of what actions we would take to improve those situations."

Picking up the point, Satterthwaite reminded the group about the lousy evaluations they had received from the staff. Virtually every discipline was found wanting.

But Hayter didn't want to get sidetracked into another angst-ridden session on the agency's faults. He tried to steer the conversation back to the larger issue.

"Well, where we left off last time is asking ourselves what business are we in? Are we in the ideas business? If you're a creative powerhouse in the ideas business you need the big idea. You've got to be able to be the company that delivers the big one."

But most clients don't think of Vickers & Benson that way, Philp argued. "They think of us as 'the agency,' there to create ads for them when they are needed and little more."

"We are an advertising agency!" Bell exclaimed, getting hot under the collar. "That's how we're listed. That's what we do. That's what we practise. That's the drawing card. I don't think we're seen as practising our basic disciplines at a level that will allow you to believe we could take on anything else. I love the notion of big ideas, but I don't think that's ownable."

Hayter rallied to the challenge. "If you're in the business of big ideas, the most important thing is the idea," he argued. "You don't have to be the dominant force. A big idea can become bigger through having the capability to excel in several dimensions.

"If you develop the big idea," he added, "it will work in any form of communication. You may decide that one is a more effective use of the dollars to deliver the big idea. My definition of a big idea is an idea that can go anywhere."

"Well I'm in support of that," Bell retorted. "That is the basic currency of what we do. I don't understand why we debate that. That is the basic currency by which the future in this business will be won or lost, I think. It is your ability to solve problems, which equals 'big idea.'"

It was Hayter's turn to look perplexed. "I'm not sure what you're saying, so I'm not going to say what I think you said. The ground for being the 'big idea' company is empty.

"I think people go out there and wing it. I think most of the work we see right now is ill-conceived, short term and 'run it as fast as it can go' for all the wrong reasons."

The discussion was quickly becoming a debate between the two men sitting at opposite ends of the conference table. The others in the room followed the match like a tennis game.

"I don't think the work that you're seeing out there is a result of them not pursuing the big idea," Bell said. "I think it's a result of them ultimately not selling the big idea. The big idea may be back on the floor somewhere. A client didn't buy the big idea, didn't believe in the big idea. And so they ran the fourth-biggest idea."

Philp could no longer sit still. "I've recently become convinced," he said, "that we are talking about what we should be. The real issue is how do we become that? In other words, I doubt they're having this conversation at Chiat/Day." (This reference was to one of the city's better-known creative hotshops.)

"Or at Geoffrey B. Roche," added Bell, referring to another agency, Geoffrey B. Roche & Partners Advertising, which had recently won a spate of awards with a billboard campaign for the Royal Ontario Museum. The ads combined pictures of the museum's own artifacts with punning copy. For example, above a mummy in a richly decorated sarcophagus ran the headline: "Bored Stiff? Come to the Museum."

Roche had started the company after quitting Chiat/Day, where he was the creative director.

Chiat/Day had also won numerous awards for such advertisers as Nissan Canada and Canadian Airlines—the client whose ads Bell had criticized at MacLaren:Lintas.

Both the Roche agency and Chiat/Day were simultaneously revered and ridiculed in the often bitchy Toronto ad community. There was criticism of what some saw as derivative work designed only to impress the judges at awards competitions.

One of the most savage detractors was Gary Prouk, chairman and national creative director of Scali McCabe Sloves.

Prouk is best remembered as the creator of a legendary TV commercial for Caramilk chocolate bars that ran in the 1970s. It featured a Mona Lisa lookalike taking a bite of the gooey confection—resulting, of course, in that famous enigmatic smile.

In private, Prouk is cultured and erudite, befitting a man so smitten with Oscar Wilde that he has amassed the finest private collection in Canada of the Irish writer's work.

But in public, Prouk could be a tiger. He regularly gave full vent to his barbed wit in the Letters to the Editor sections of the trade papers. He saved his most caustic comments for Roche, a one-time employee.

When asked by *Toronto Life* magazine in 1993 to assess Roche's work, Prouk let loose with venomous abandon.

"It's a smart-ass school of advertising, very mannered," he said about Roche. "Even when he worked for me he was very magpie-ish, always studying other people's stuff, soaking it all up. I once said: 'At the moment of his death, someone else's life will flash in front of him.'

"I don't believe we as an industry should be so slavishly awarding, and rewarding, work that is overtly precocious. It's not hard to do what Roche does; 19-year-old art school kids do this kind of stuff, you know. It's like waving your pee-pee around in print."

But even the cattiest of the carpers had to envy Roche and Chiat/Day for their uncanny ability to win accounts, create memorable ads and grab headlines.


O'Malley, who had been a mute witness to the wrangling among his colleagues, startled the group by speaking up.

"I think it comes down to right where John started," he said softly. "That's what I was interested in. The definition of the idea. I've been hearing different definitions.

"The big idea for McDonald's might be, I don't know, a seventy-nine-cent Big Mac. That's a big idea. Everything stems from that. That's what we're here to do. It might be a new product. That's the advantage of the spinning circles," he said, pointing to Hayter's easel drawing. "We all bring a different dimension to it."

"You've got to have the people who are capable of generating the big ideas," Bell reiterated.

"Maybe we've got one or two big ideas for our clients that can go on for a long time," Hayter answered. "You can take it in any direction, in any medium. You can change the execution but the idea stays. And the idea is so big that the client has an advantage over its competitors because it just connects with its customers."

"Give us an idea," Bell asked of Hayter.

"I think the Bank of Montreal's 'We're Paying Attention' campaign is a big idea," he replied. "I think it has the potential to grow and become bigger and better."

"I'm not talking about what we are," he added. "I'm not talking about whether we have the capability. I'm saying where do we have to be five years from now, and ten years from now, to survive? And if we aim at it, manage our way through, I think we'll have a better chance than anybody in this industry.

"I think the opportunity for us to go into the ground where no one's been is boundary-less. And we have an advantage over anybody else because first of all we are private, we are one office and we are talking about it."

"I for one don't disagree with that at all," Philp chimed in. "The 'stuck' place for me is that's the top of the benefit pyramid, and I think if you talk to clients in general terms about what they want from an agency I think the two predominant themes you get, expressed one way or another, are: We want people sitting across the table who are smarter than we are in a marketing communications sense; and we want supreme executional competence.

"If you can build on that the kind of thing you're talking about—" He broke off, momentarily stymied. "I'm just having a hard time getting my head into the high-level stuff you're getting at."

By this point, even Hayter was starting to get lost in all the verbiage about creative powerhouses, big ideas, empowerment and centres of excellence.

He tried to start again. He walked over to the easel and drew a box around the word "inventors." Underneath, he drew five long boxes to represent different agency departments, the so-called centres of excellence.

"I think you need the inventors," he said, brandishing his marker. "All they work on are creating the big ideas. They may only work on twelve a year or fifteen a year. But that's their job. They invent the big ideas. They don't execute them. The only client time they have is selling the big idea."

He pointed the marker at each centre of excellence. "And over here you have another team, and another team, and you keep building those teams. You may even develop another group of inventors."

McCormick, who had been growing progressively irritated, gave sudden voice to his discontent.

"That ivory tower concept bugs me," he snapped. "I think there are different kinds of big ideas. I think there are strategic big ideas, creative big ideas. I think there are production big ideas. I don't see how you could fit all of those disciplines in this élite club of inventors up there."

Bell picked up McCormick's gauntlet. "That's the model for a classic creative department," he said. "That's what creative directors do. But we don't have, currently, the creative directors at this agency. So we're not filling that mandate, because that's basically what their role is. You manage the creative resource to come up with the big ideas."

Now it was Satterthwaite's turn to get agitated.

"I don't know a creative department in this country—I'm probably wrong but I don't know of one—that says the first thing we're going to do is come up with a big idea and have a lot of people working on lots of big ideas."

"Wait a second, hold on," Bell said. "I think the danger is we think just because we want a big idea we're going to get one."

Turning to O'Malley, he added, "I think it was you once who said three times in your career you're going to see a big idea. In your career!"

"Do you believe we should deliver to each client the biggest idea in their category?" Hayter asked Bell.

"I think we should deliver the biggest idea the best people we have are capable of delivering," Bell answered. "You're not going to hit home runs every time. There's a risk of over-taxing this notion of a big idea so that it loses meaning."

Hayter pushed his point. "Do you think that a definition for a big idea is delivering to our clients the most relevant strategy and most compelling delivery of that strategy in its category? I think that's an attainable goal, and that's my definition of a big idea."

McCormick still wasn't convinced. "It's a radical way of organizing an agency, though," he muttered. Why spend so much time talking about big ideas? Why not just get on with it?

The others, however, weren't ready to let the matter drop.

Bell again: "If you get the best people in direct marketing, the best people in the creative department, the best account people, the best production people, the best broadcast production people, I think your chances of generating the big idea go up a whole lot from where we are now."

"All right," Hayter agreed. "I think we know that we have to improve our talent base from top to bottom. I don't think we need to spend a lot of time on that. How do we organize? How do we structure?"

"What we're talking about here is a pretty fundamental cultural change," Philp said. "So the question is, is it possible to do that wholesale? Can you do that throughout the organziation?"

"Do you want a reaction to that?" Hayter asked.

"I don't know what the answer is myself."

Hayter did. "I think you've got to agree about the organizational structure, and then you've got to assign people at the top to lead it. You've got to find within each organizational unit the players, the champions, the producers. Those you can count on. You empower them and then you identify the areas where you've got to make absolutely necessary changes now and then as you go you manage and evolve change as you can afford—financially, from an organizational team concept and from a client concept."

"So you create a framework throughout the organization where it can happen," Satterthwaite said. "But you recognize there are certain areas where it must happen as a priority."

"It's all in the process," Hayter assured him. "The group that is in this room today is very different than the group that was in here a year and a half ago. It's at work. We're talking about things we didn't talk about a year and a half ago."

The point was, he added, that the group had yet to really agree on what the agency's mandate should be.

"Where isn't the vision currently shared?" Philp asked.

"I'm not so sure it's shared here," Hayter replied, looking about the room.

Bell threw up his hands. "If it is not yet shared, there's the problem! If it is shared here, then the task is to make sure that it's bought into out there," he said, nodding to the door and the agency's staff beyond.

"But that's why I was pushing for an agreement on the business we're in, and the definition of being known as Canada's creative powerhouse," Hayter said. "Because you have to have a measure of that that you all agree on. My measure of that, and the reason I was pushing for it, is the best work in our client's category is done by us. And that's our goal. We may not be there all the time, but every goddamn time we get down and think and are challenged, we challenge ourselves to get there."

"Okay," Bell said. "If it needs to be said, we should put it down on paper and say it. I can't think of how I would work under any other mindset."

"You think that way," Hayter said. "I don't know how many others think that way. I don't know how many people come in here and say 'I passionately come in here every day and I drive myself to accomplish that.' Very few."

Philp was anxious to get back to basics. Few could doubt that being a creative powerhouse was a worthy goal. But what about the mandate of doing only the best work in a category? Would principle stand before profit?

"Even if it means there are certain businesses we don't go after?" he asked. "Even if it means we won't always make the kind of profit margin as last year? Or even if it means that we're going to lose some business? Or even if it means this is going to become a less pleasant place to work in?"

Hayter reminded him about the decision to stop working for the Ontario Lottery Corporation over a matter of principle, because the agency disagreed with the OLC's policy of awarding lottery projects on a piecemeal basis.

"Last year we walked away from the Ontario Lottery," he said. "A very gutsy thing. Our profit margins were slim, but we did it. We've made some tough calls."

"To get people to buy into it, they have to sense a consistency of the message," Bell said. "The calls that we make have to address 'creative powerhouse'—if that is the way we're going to fly. We are not going to go out, in spite of the fact that they spend $20 million a year, and take on The Brick, if we feel The Brick will not fulfil our mission. That's the ethical call that will have to be made. We have to make the call that says 'this is antithetical to our goal and our mission.'"

"And building on that point," added Philp, "I would argue that if we really believed in the mission our first priority wouldn't in fact be new business at all."

More important would be carefully managing the agency's growth, assuming that growth would come slowly.

"I agree with that," Hayter said. "That was our goal. That has been our goal. We have not aggressively pursued new business. We have worked very hard at building our product and our customer relationships. And it's paying off. And I think consistently our work is getting better. And I think it will continue to improve. We're being able to develop ideas that are daring, bold and being bought by clients that wouldn't have bought them a year ago.

"I think Quaker is now willing, through the Gatorade work, to look at us very differently, and our work very differently. We continue to build with the Bank of Montreal. Our work on the Ontario Jockey Club is going to be a hell of a lot better than it has been."

He paused. "So back to Bruce, and your question 'where do we go from here?' I gave you my thoughts. Anybody else got any comments? If we want to be the definition of Canada's creative powerhouse, how do we get there? What do we do differently?"

McCormick, the direct-mail man, took a tangent and launched into a topic dear to his heart: the death of mass media as the preferred marketing strategy. The majority of spending was now being allocated to alternative communications. Advertising was a dying art. TV audiences were too fragmented for the shotgun approach of the past. Target marketing was the new religion.

Bell, the advertising maven, sneered. "The 500-channel 'Death Star,' right? You've got people sold a giant bill of goods. Do you think I'm really going to feel good about coming home one day after advertising is 'dead' and seeing six-hundred direct-mail pieces shoved in my fucking door?"

McCormick gave it right back. "Pick up *Fortune* or *Business Week* or any of those. Every ad that's in there is a direct marketing ad. Every one. Almost all business-to-business communication—any type—is now direct marketing. Turn on CNN television. Just sit and watch it for eight hours. Count the number of direct-marketing television commercials. Notice how I haven't said one fucking word about direct mail yet?"

And what about all those half-hour infomercials (commercials masquerading as legitimate news programs)? "That whole area is going to be so vast and we're sitting here talking about fucking advertising, which is shrinking all over the world!"

Philp, the mediator, jumped in. "Advertising is going to assume certain specific roles in the marketing mix," he said reasonably. "It used to do everything. It's not going to do everything any more. It's going to do a couple of things. And direct marketing will do a couple of things."

McCormick was not be put off by compromise. "In-bound telemarketing is doing huge things," he said. "People make the fucking call because they want to. Like Pizza Pizza. It's the best telemarketing campaign I've ever seen. They made their whole message their phone number!"

"I think those people who are going to be ahead of the curve are the ones who figure out how to use those [marketing alternatives] in the best possible way," Philp replied. "That's what we have to be good at."

"How do we manage that?" Hayter asked.

"We keep doing what we're doing, just do it better, which is one way," Satterthwaite answered. "I've got to believe we're interested in talking about more than that."

"How might we do things differently?" Hayter asked again.

"I happen to buy into something like what John described," Philp answered, getting to the inventors group. "Except that I don't see these guys as sheltered people. If I was reorganizing the agency along this model, these guys wouldn't be hidden behind the scenes."

They wouldn't, Hayter said. But neither would they have to contend with the "administrivia" of managing people. "They're worried about the big idea that drives the business."

To which Satterthwaite asked: "How might we organize ourselves differently, recognizing that we have a lot of clients that want process management, and some that don't? And increasing numbers don't. How might we do things differently that's going to help bring this alive with something that's credible and makes sense and we can produce?"

"It just struck me now during this conversation," Philp broke in, "that it may be theoretically possible to design one structure that suits both kinds of customers."

He added: "As a strategic objective it would be interesting to go through our current client list and effectively write account plans that are aimed at weaning clients off the process."

Hayter saw headway being made.

"I don't know if I'm dreaming," he said, "but I would love to believe that each account is going to have a team of people who bring different things to the party."

He paused. "How do we organize so that we can put a fucking armada against an idea when we need to? You don't need it on everything. Obviously if you're doing a tray-liner it's a one-person job and they're great at it, and if you've got the best guy or person and they're passionate about delivering the best tray-liner, you're going to get the best tray-liner.

"But the armada against the big idea pushes as high and wide as you can. We have it on Gatorade. Everybody knows who the players are."

"We don't have an armada pushing for the big idea," Satterthwaite corrected him. "We developed an integrated communications plan that involved several disciplines and you," he turned to Bell, "were called upon to do your part. But no force was called upon to come up with the big idea that would be inherent in the product."

"I want to challenge the whole armada notion for a minute," Philp said, "because I believe in these ad hoc team things. I also believe there's really a diminishing return putting too many resources against an idea. The best ideas that have ever come out of this place have had their genesis in a tight group, a small group or even a pair."

"Or an individual," Bell added. "And they were executed by an armada who got it, who understood."

"I don't have a problem with that," Hayter said. "Sometimes the armada will include everybody in developing the big idea, if it's a last-minute thing or a new business presentation."

"This notion of pursuing the big idea isn't just 'well, let's have a meeting and state the need for a big idea and then come back three days from now with a big idea,'" Bell continued. "You've got to have the time for the big minds to generate that thinking. If what we're doing is leaving the meeting where we've declared the need for a big idea on behalf of a client and then all we do is spend the next seventy-two hours working on other pieces of business, no wonder we're not coming up with the big ideas.

"So the process is really killing us. If we believe in a notion called the brain trust and we trust that those people really love what they do, we should be seeing a lot of this." He raised his feet to the table, crossed them and sat back.

"You should be going by offices and seeing a lot of silence."

Hayter nodded. "I think all of us spend probably two to three times the amount of time we should be spending on non-work.

"The only time I think," he added, "is away from the office."

"I spend a lot of time with my people," Philp said. "Fifteen-minute hallway meetings and a lot of advice and crisis intervention and all that kind of stuff. If only we could cut that in half."

Murmurs of agreement around the table.

"I think we organize to drive out process, and we build centres of excellence," Hayter said. "That reassigns everybody in this room, because it's got to begin with us. I believe if our end is to, with every client, have the best work and the best idea in their category, we have to have a core strategic group, an ideas group. And, since it's just a few people, it means that group can only take on certain assignments initially."

He looked around the room. "I don't know if we shouldn't just end for today. And we'll all agree on our process for the next meeting. And that will become the framework for which we go forward."

Philp went up the easel to summarize the goals the group had set in the meeting. On a fresh sheet of paper he wrote: AGREED SO FAR.

"The measure of being a creative powerhouse will be that we deliver the category's best work for each of our clients," Hayter said. "At the end of the day, everybody has to say, 'Have we or have we not delivered the best category work?'"

Philp wrote: CREATIVE POWERHOUSE—CATEGORY'S BEST MAR-KETING COMMUNICATIONS FOR EVERY CLIENT.

Next point. "We've agreed that we must remove process and admin-istrivia," Hayter offered.

"Reduce," Satterthwaite corrected him. "It's different than remove."

"Yes," Hayter agreed. "Because you're never going to remove it entirely."

"See, when you were talking," Philp said, "I was going to write we were going to get out of the process business."

"I think it's one of those things like McDonald's' '100 per cent cus-tomer satisfaction'—even though they recognize it's unattainable," Hayter explained. "It's a pursuit of it. They're always trying to get there and get there and get there. And they set measurable results. Unless we have something here we can measure against we won't get there. So I'd like to have it quantifiable. So maybe we go back and say 'to eliminate unnecessary process that gets in the way of our achieving our vision of becoming a creative powerhouse.' So that's the goal.

"You may decide, Mike," he said, nodding to the direct-marketer, "that 70 per cent of your time is 'process' and administrivia and you want to get it to 20 per cent. You have your own personal plan to do that."

With that, Philp wrote down the second goal. WE WANT TO ELIMI-NATE PROCESS THAT DOESN'T LEAD TO—and he drew an arrow to the first goal—CREATIVE POWERHOUSE.

"We need to reorganize or restructure the agency to put that in place," Hayter said. "I think we agree that we must develop strategies for the centres of excellence. How we bring the centres of excellence together to accomplish 'creative powerhouse.' The issue is not centres of excellence. The issue is how we deploy it."

There was a long silence.

"I think we agreed that we had to deploy our best talent resources in a way in which we can kick-start the move towards the vision of 'creative powerhouse,'" he reminded them again.

"I don't think the big idea is bigger than advertising or direct marketing or media. I do believe, however, that the people who can consistently deliver powerful ideas are few and far between, and initially as a way of marshalling and deploying our best talent we may need a core central group.

"Then, if our goal is to go beyond that and broaden that so that we're not dependent on a few people, we go find them. But there aren't a thousand of them out there. I believe there are maybe thirty or a hundred—but they're not out there in the thousands.

"I've been in this business for thirty years. I could name you a handful I've run into. Maybe two handfuls, but not hundreds of very good people who could take an idea and make it exciting and clever. But what I'm talking about is the big ideas. That insight that says, 'Oh shit, can I play with this—I can take this so far!' As opposed to, 'What the fuck is this? I don't know what to do with this!'

"I'm not talking about a line of copy or a piece of advertising. I'm talking about that little thing that could get the Molson people excited when they come in. And they walk out of here saying, 'I'm emotionally drained by the size of that idea, the challenge and the implications it has for our business. I'm just fucking wild!'

"That's what I'm talking about. And that started with a little piece of paper that had a couple of little things on it. And then the magic is easier because there was something there to work with."

Philp then wrote down the third goal: WE WILL ORGANIZE AROUND CENTRES OF EXCELLENCE. Underneath, he wrote the fourth: WE NEED STRATEGIES FOR EACH ONE, AND A STRATEGY FOR BRINGING THEM TOGETHER.

"Talking about what we've agreed, you just talked about the power of an idea," Satterthwaite said to Hayter. "That could be summarized in a sentence."

"We've all agreed the most powerful thing we can bring to our clients is the big idea, have we not?" Hayter asked. "So what I tried to do was define what a big idea was, because the definition of a big idea we've agreed to is something that gives the client a category best. In other words, when they put that on the air that is working harder for them than a competitor's work."

Philp wrote: WE NEED A WAY TO DEPLOY OUR BEST TALENT TO LEAD THE WAY.

Not surprisingly, by this point the group was getting edgy, weary from going around in circles. No one was really sure what in fact they had agreed to. Once again, the talk turned to 'big idea' versus 'category best.' Which was the real corporate objective?

"My definition of an idea," Satterthwaite said, "is one that has the legs to go across the board and work on everything."

But was there enough money in the budget to hire the right people to accomplish that? McCormick doubted there was.

"They can be got," Hayter reassured him. "It's not easy, but it can be done."

That still didn't answer the question of what exactly a big idea was. Rumbles of disagreement circulated through the room.

Hayter decided it was time to call a halt. "I think we've gone past ideas," he said. "Our goal is to deliver to each client the best work in its category. Some of it is going to be way up there, and some is not going to be as high, obviously. But as long as we strive to do the best. And everybody knows when they say, 'What am I here to deliver?' they can say, 'I am here to deliver the best work. And you know what? I haven't fucking done it. But I'm going to do something about it.'

"Or they can say, 'I've done it.' The Bank of Montreal—we've done it but, boy, are we being challenged, and we're going to have to kick our butts to dial it up and really get at it to stay there because everybody else is out there after us.

"That kind of personal measurement and that kind of personal honesty is what drives us."

With that, the meeting seemed ready to end. Hayter suggested they get out their daytimers to pick a date for the next meeting. While they were comparing schedules, Bell continued to worry aloud.

"You can do the category's best work and it can still be a piece of shit," he said. "It's void of any suitable standards. In the category of drugstores, in terms of the work that's been done, you're good by acclamation basically because everybody else is bad."

Why the fuss? McCormick asked. Why not just say the goal is to do the "best job we could possibly do?"

"I don't buy that," Hayter answered him. "Because I think right now a lot of us would say we're doing the best job we can do. But we're doing a below average job for a hundred different reasons. We've got to eliminate that."

"Well, let's find out what the reasons are and eliminate them," McCormick said.

Hayter got up from his chair and left the room. He returned a few moments later with a sheet of paper.

"I wrote this down this morning," he said. "It's not right, but this is what I had. I didn't want to come in here and sell what I had, I wanted to keep this open. The vision is 'be known as Canada's creative powerhouse.' What I had was: 'The company that is driven to create and execute campaign ideas'—I like the 'driven' word, because it's got the passion we talked about—'which gives clients an identifiable market-place advantage.'

"'Identifiable' may be too loose. And I think it should say something like 'individually and collectively we are driven to.'"

"I feel like we're taking this giant step backwards," Bell interrupted. "Maybe it's just me today or my mood or whatever, but I feel like we're losing the focus. I think we're talking about big, big, big, big stuff. And you don't need to talk about big stuff! I think we need to talk about how the work has got to get better in every single discipline.

"We should come in next time with five suggestions from each of us on how to make that work better. And let's get on with it."

"That's not good enough," Hayter shot back. "It's vague. We've got to have something that we invest against, we organize against, and people can stand up and say: 'All of a sudden it's fucking clear!'"

"I think we're doing what you said now. Part of the problem is that we as an organization are not tight on where we're going. And unless we're tight and we all share that, we ain't going to get there."

Bell stood his ground. "I think what we're talking about is going after the Stanley Cup," he said. "But what we should be talking about is how to skate better. I don't think we know how to skate well enough to even think about making the playoffs. I think we should learn how to skate and then maybe worry about how to win the Stanley Cup. We're going to wear ourselves out with this."

"I'm tired of being wishy-washy," Hayter said angrily.

"So am I," Bell shot back.

"I want to get us focused and I want to get us aimed at something," Hayter insisted. "What we keep stumbling on is, we said we want to be Canada's powerhouse. But I want a definition of what Canada's pow-erhouse is going to be so that everybody in this place knows exactly what it is."

"I'm right behind you," Philp said to Hayter. "I think it's going to be the sum total of all the parts. But my head is back at how I can make my part get me where you're going."

"Exactly," Bell said.

"But I'm there," Philp continued. "I'm on the same page and I want to go to the same place."

"I don't think you have to make it loftier than what it is," Bell said. "We'll be Canada's creative powerhouse. How are you going to do that? Here's how I'm going to do it. Boom, boom, boom, boom, boom. Five ways, let's go." He turned to Philp. "How are you going to do it? Here's his contribution to that mission. Boom, boom, boom, boom, boom."

He nodded to the others. "Same with you. Same with you. And we're on the road! And the jury will be out and hopefully will come in with a verdict in another year or whatever and say, 'These guys are doing it.' I don't think it has to be any loftier than that."

"And I'm talking about how you get there!" Hayter exploded. "I do agree having these centres of excellence is a strategy that has to be developed. Each centre has got to be powerful. But we've got to come together as an organization. We better know how we play together, how we interchange, how we interact. And unless we do that we're going to continue to wander. And right now this place is like a bowl of jelly! We've got to do much better than that.

"The kinds of things we talked about up there, both organizationally and structurally, I think are critical to the delivery of the centres of excellence. And I don't think we step away from it. As difficult as it is, as painful as it is, you got to stay on it and we've got to see it through.

"And every day I expect you, each of us, to deliver against coming up with the biggest idea we can on every piece of business. But I think just to leave this and go and not pull it all together—"Jesus Christ! It would probably be a disaster."

Bell was unbowed. "I tell you, I swear to God, there are not people out there that are screaming for some Biblical mission," he said. "They are not. They're screaming for day-to-day leadership of this place. They're not screaming for some long-term vision. They're not doing it!

"I don't think the clients are either. I don't think our prospective clients are. I think what they're looking for is excellence on a day-to-day basis from what we do."

Take the current Vickers & Benson mission statement, Bell snapped, stabbing the air in front of a framed sign hanging on the wall to his right. It was the agency's motto, printed like a poem:

> Everyday, in every way,
> to build our clients' business
> we must empower one another to:
> Make it creative.
> Make it impactful.
> Make it an advantage.
> Make it successful.
> V&B
> People Given The Power
> To Make It Happen.

How many employees could recite it? Bell asked the group. Why not something more succinct, punchier? Something that would really rally the troops.

"The frustration I've had so far today," he began, "is that I'm hearing motherhood statements—"

"Fine," Hayter broke in. "But the point that you raised, and the point that I disagree with very strongly, is if we're going to eliminate process from this business so that you can get on with what you want to do and everybody wants to do, we've got to reorganize and rethink this business. And I don't think it's as simple as 'everybody go away and think about their own centre of excellence.'

"I think it's one thing we do. As we said, if we organize around centres of excellence, then we need strategies for each one. I agree with that. But how we pull this company together—how we pull together—is as important as are centres of excellence. And right now we ain't pulling it together!"

Hayter stood up to signal the meeting was over. The others shuffled their papers, rose groggily from the table and straggled through the glass-panelled doors into the corridor beyond.

They walked stiffly, like aging jocks winded by one too many overtime plays, dreading the prospect of one more round before the game could be called.

# CHAPTER 4

WHILE THE MANAGERS feuded over Vickers & Benson's future, there was still the matter of the day-to-day operation of the agency to contend with. There were clients to be serviced, accounts to be pitched and ads to be created.

A priority was a new campaign for Heineken, a brand Molson Breweries distributes in Canada through its Santa Fe Beverage division. It fell to Bell and art director Larry Gordon to come up with a new series of ads to stimulate sales in the coming summer beer season.

It was a project both partners loved. It was high profile and it was also a lot of fun. Like the day the two got caught up in a laughing fit. As they were playing around with ideas, they struck on what they thought was a dynamite concept: a sheep—make that a black sheep—in full surfing gear, baggy trunks, sunglasses and all. That would certainly spruce up Heineken's stodgy Dutch-brewed, premium-priced image. Make it a little silly and do away with pretention.

But then the mental skids came on. Wouldn't a surfing sheep trivialize what was, after all, one of the most famous international brands in the world? Besides, it really wasn't on strategy, was it? John Boniface, the agency's group director on Heineken, said make it contemporary, not slapstick.

With a sigh and one last giggle, Bell and Gordon went back to the drawing board.

Boniface, one of the agency's top account men, pored over the research to see why Heineken, arguably one of the most revered brands in the beer industry, had fallen on such hard times. Certainly that wasn't always the case.

There was a time when Heineken was the imported beer that all others were measured against. Aficionados relished its somewhat bitter, European flavour. Fans of design excellence treasured the green bottle with its distinctive label. Those who wanted to impress their mates ordered it in trendy bars.

Until the early 1980s, Heineken didn't have any real competition in the upscale import category. It was either Heineken or one of the domestic brews sold in humdrum standard stubby brown bottles.

But that all changed in 1983, when Carling O'Keefe, now part of Molson Breweries, brought out Miller High Life in clear, private-mould bottles. Its immediate success spawned numerous imitators as the other major brewers stampeded to introduce their own licensed products in custom bottle and can formats.

As the decade progressed, microbrewers began hitting the store shelves with domestic brands made with pure ingredients and no additives, preservatives and stabilizers. Those who appreciated quality flocked to these new labels, prompting the major brewers to fight back with an ever-lengthening list of specialty beers. They started with light versions of their most popular sellers, then launched whole new categories.

The brand proliferation reached its zenith in early 1993, when both Labatt's and Molson introduced ice beers to add to their rosters of dry, bottled draught and non-alcoholic brews.

Then in the summer of 1993, the stalemate in an acrimonious tussle between Canada and the United States was resolved when it was agreed Canada would allow foreign beers to be freely sold in provincial beer stores. In return, price sanctions against Canadian brewers were to be dropped by the Americans.

The anticipation of an onslaught of cheap, U.S. suds forced the Canadians to introduce bargain-priced beers of their own. In July, Molson launched an entire family of products under its cut-rate Carling label. Labatt's countered with Wildcat. Loblaw's, the king of private-label products, got into the act with a number of beers under its President's Choice banner. Brew-your-own outlets began rising up in the suburbs like brewer's yeast.

Against this backdrop of continuous new-product innovation and introduction, total beer sales remained stubbornly flat. Consumers had altered their imbibing habits, buying less beer as concerns about health and fitness, and drinking and driving, came to the fore. Steadily rising taxes on beer and other alcoholic beverages only worsened the sales picture.

Heineken, meanwhile, once the gold standard of beers, was losing even more ground. Its sales were dropping faster than industry averages. Part of the blame was the lack of product promotion. By the time Boniface sat down to write a creative brief for Bell and Gordon, the brand had received virtually no advertising support for almost two years, and its top-of-mind awareness among consumers had plummeted.

However, Heineken remained Canada's top-selling non-U.S. import, although Mexico's Corona brand was closing the gap. There were no problems with the perceived quality of the product, nor with its credentials as a quality brew, nor its distribution.

In other words, Boniface concluded, there was no rational reason why the brand was faltering. Why then wasn't it still prospering?

Boniface identified four key factors.

First, the brand had lost its topicality. It used to be talked about. It had tradition working in its favour, an aura of superiority.

Second, the brand appeared to have gone into hiding. The lack of promotion made it look as though Heineken had surrendered to its rivals in the domestic and imported specialty niche market.

The third factor, tied to the second, was the perception that Heineken had nothing new to say; that it had lost its relevancy, the unique properties that made it the gold standard.

Finally, it was no longer the brand young drinkers looked up to. While the tradition was there, it was not perceived as a beer to aspire to.

The challenge as far as Boniface could determine was to maintain Heineken's heritage, and at the same time revitalize the brand's unique selling proposition as a distinctive alternative to the also-rans and wannabes. The goal was to build sales over both the short and long terms.

In his brief to Bell and Gordon, he said the advertising should talk to the heart, and the head would follow. Avoid focusing on specific occasions and highlight the "moods" that made ordering a Heineken special.

The brand characteristics to be extolled touched on a number of product attributes, ranging from quality and tradition to craftsmanship and brand familiarity. The ads should be intelligent, humorous, approachable and passionate.

Downplay any semblance of élitism or eighties-style Yuppieness. Don't be trendy or dated. And most important, don't be boring.

Using a spokesperson would be too limiting to hit the wide demographic target. Remember that the Heineken drinker is, at least attitudinally, a contemporary thinker who eschews materialistic trappings. So don't make it snooty.

Present Heineken as an intriguing brand that has character, that is simple, successful and consistent. In other words, a beer for the 1990s.

Bell and Gordon took Boniface's brief and began brainstorming. It wasn't long before they nailed the problem. The brand, they figured, had lost much of its allure in the greatly expanded beer universe. It had simply been forgotten.

A couple of days into the project, Gordon hit the bull's-eye. The brand had lost its "sexiness." It once was seen as desirable, contemporary and fashionable. Those days and that aura were gone.

They set out to bring some of that magic back. They wanted to ignite the consciousness of a new generation of beer drinkers, and remind lapsed customers why they once valued the brand.

Even before they started work devising the campaign, they knew they would not play up Dutch brewmasters, wooden shoes and other travelogue images that a brand like Heineken could conjure. Today's drinker just didn't care about that when Canadian microbrewers could claim they too adhered to age-old traditions of beer making. In the final analysis, being imported was important, but not that important.

So Bell and Gordon took a different tack.

"We made a couple of real false starts," Bell conceded. "We wanted to bring about change quickly."

Perhaps too quickly. In their zeal to drive up sales, they conspired to create ads that positioned Heineken as the beer of choice for the summer.

The idea was to taunt beer drinkers with the shortness of the season. Make the best of it, their ads admonished. Drink the best beer. Drink Heineken.

That's when the black sheep entered the picture, as an off-the-wall call to seize the moment. Another execution showed a woman standing on a dock, a Heineken in hand. The copy would read something like: "Look at it this way. In another 56 days you will have lost your tan and your teeth will be chattering. Make the best of it." *Carpe diem* with Heineken.

It was a cheeky direction, one they soon realized fell short of the mark. That strategy could apply to just about any beer, even domestic brews. It didn't say enough about the attributes peculiar to Heineken.

"The error in that is you end up selling the soup du jour," Bell said. "It becomes really short-term thinking. We do a great job at positioning this beer as the beer this summer. But what happens come October? It's over. And we're talking about one of the great beer icons.

"We had to remind ourselves that what we're talking about is one of the great names in beer, one of the truly big global brands, and it deserved to have something that was larger than this one-off, seasonal kind of approach."

They agreed that the "summer" campaign lacked substance to work over the long haul. It had the right amount of cheek, but it was just too "fluffy."

"It wasn't big enough," Bell said. "It didn't last long enough. It didn't go the distance." It was cotton-candy advertising that was immediately likeable and easily consumed, but ultimately unfulfilling.

So they dug deeper. They argued over coffee and cigarettes at the local cafe, compared notes at the restaurant downstairs from their offices. Then one day the answer just came.

"We started in our own minds defining situations or moments where Heineken would be right, where Heineken would be a unique fit," Gordon said. "We started realizing in fact that you're not going to pick up a twelve-pack of Heineken and go party with the boys. But there are other moments, standing on a dock at a cottage watching a sunset or contemplating life, when a Heineken is very much a fit.

"We didn't want to do, necessarily, advertising that was just directed at moments of usage. But what it did was get our heads around what the moments are. You get around what the moments are, you get into the mindset of 'why Heineken?' Why should I get a Heineken? Why should I feel like a Heineken?"

It wasn't a far leap from that rationale to the creative team's development of what Bell was to tag "Heineken haikus." Each moment that could be classified as having the requisite uniqueness that only ordering a Heineken could satisfy became the subject of a brief poetic invocation.

"What we came down to was these are essentially right moments," Gordon said. "In fact, 'essentially right' is the line that closed every piece of communication for Heineken."

Bell loved the line. "As soon as we hit that, we knew we were there," he said. "The bullshit detector was: Are these moments essentially right? Did you feel that they were moments that have a genuine, authentic feel surrounding them that you could envision this beer being a part of?"

The partners went into a frenzy of writing. They wrote twenty-five, thirty different scenarios, each one deemed essentially right for drinking Heineken beer. A big, bold colour picture of a Heineken bottle would dominate each ad.

Both contributed equally to writing the ads, even though Bell was nominally the copywriter and Gordon the art director. That was typical of their working style, Bell said.

"In 99.99 per cent of the stuff that Larry and I do, I lose touch with who does what. I think that's what works extremely well with us. We do stuff together. I think some of the best stuff we've done from a writing standpoint has come from Larry.

"Occasionally I make a contribution art directorially," he added as a modest aside.

The "haikus" flew from their pencils. Among them:

"You read and watch. She does her toes." "Bar band. 2000 people. A whisper in your ear." "The Bulls. The jazz. Big screen. Large pizza." One they toyed with, but ultimately rejected, was: "A ceiling fan. A siesta. A friend."

Both men had their favourites. For Gordon it was "Thunderstorm. Screened Porch. *Sunday Times.*" Bell's was "Smokey sax. Her body in your shirt."

Each ended with the signature line "Heineken. Essentially right." There would be no visuals explaining the text. It would be up to the imagination of the reader to interpret what the "haikus" really meant. If one execution proved inscrutable, that would be all right. Perhaps the next one would hit home.

The hoped-for cumulative effect would be that here was a beer that wasn't afraid to be intellectually provocative. One that felt at ease speaking personally. One that was a bit saucy, witty but never patronizing.

"Much of what we were creating was designed to have these intimate little moments that weren't sexual, but they were sensual," Bell said. "People who would consume this beer were not always hanging out with the guys. It was not a party-time brew."

Two weeks after they sat down to blue-sky the campaign, Bell and Gordon presented the lot to Ted Mealing, area export manager for Heineken.

Mealing wasn't too sure exactly what to make of the "essentially right" positioning tag-line, but he trusted the creative team's judgment. Go with it, he said, giving his blessing.

There was only one more hitch before the ads could be posted on billboards and subway cars. Bell and Gordon had to get the approval of the Ontario Liquor Control Board, which vets the province's liquor ads. And the temperance-minded bureaucrats turned them down flat.

Implying that Heineken was an "essential" component for relaxing or having a good time was *verboten,* they ruled. The campaign would have to be modified. The one about "Her body, your shirt" was to be scrapped altogether.

Bell and Gordon were devastated. To salvage what they considered to be a brilliant concept, they agreed to drop the contentious line. And they decided they probably didn't need it anyway, that the "mind puzzles" were so strong that they necessarily implied episodes that were "essentially right" to be drinking Heineken. The partners had already eliminated "haikus" they felt didn't really describe a special moment.

The campaign was just as powerful, and perhaps even more so, leaving the obvious unstated.

But they decided to keep the line in reserve, just in case. If the concept was to be extended into other media down the road, "essentially right" just might pass muster.

"Had we just gone to a product shot at the end of a television commercial and said Heineken is essentially right, I doubt that there would have been a problem. So that's still open for us," Bell said.

When he and Gordon were devising the campaign, they used each other as sounding boards. They would place themselves in each "essential" moment. They figured they were as close to the target group for Heineken as anyone. They were the same well-off, male boomers the ads were hoping to reach.

Take Gordon's favourite, the "Thunderstorm" ad, for example.

"To be able to sit for an hour with a newspaper is a huge treat for me," he explained. "I have three kids, and I don't get to do that any more alone. And Heineken is a sipping beer. You're not going to throw back three or four of them at a sitting."

The same private mood exists even in the din of a nightclub, he said. "That's why a whisper in your ear is so important. Because even amongst all of this noise and stuff and energy going on, there's this quiet moment between a man and a woman."

"For me, the magic came when I saw what Larry did with the layouts," Bell said. "It was like all of a sudden it was physical. It wasn't just this Heineken haiku in words. It all of a sudden had shape and dimension to it. It was like 'Wow! This is working. This is working big time.'

"When we went to the presentation, we whipped these boards out, we put them up and it was instantaneous—as it was when Boniface came into the office and looked. Bingo. People got it."

Five executions of the concept were selected to run. Almost as soon as they were posted in subways, they began to be pilfered—the biggest compliment a creative person can receive. If people liked your ads so much they would steal them, you knew you'd scored.

Credit for that has to be shared with Boniface, who came up with the original creative brief, Gordon said.

"What the brief was telling us was you've got this really terrific, traditional, imported green bottle. Traditional label. Bitter beer. You've got all of that on the one hand. But we don't want to draw anybody's attention to any of that old baggage. It's got to be new."

Make Heineken relevant to new customers without resorting to clichés, the brief demanded. And surprise long-time fans from their apathy, to get the brand back on their shopping lists.

"My idea of Heineken hasn't changed in twenty years," Gordon said. "Guys our age, I'm sure we think of Heineken very much the same way as we used to. Maybe our advertising will get us to think about it a little more. It's not changing the way we think about Heineken. It's not supposed to."

Bill Bremner (right), the agency's late chairman, in 1989, celebrating
the tenth anniversary of Vickers & Benson's relationship with
McDonald's Restaurants of Canada Ltd. George Cohon, McDonald's
senior chairman (left) and Ronald McDonald join in the festivities.

President and chief executive John Hayter joined Vickers & Benson
in 1991 after years on the international advertising fast track.

Terry O'Malley, agency chairman and copywriter, pictured in his office. Note the marathon racing bibs on the wall behind him.

Bruce Philp, who started out as director of client services, was promoted to executive creative director in 1993.

Chief operating officer Jim Satterthwaite, a victim of
mergermania in the 1980s, was recruited by John Hayter
to be Vickers & Benson's second in command.

Terry Bell, who started his agency career in Vickers & Benson's mailroom
in the 1960s, returned to the firm in the 1990s after being fired from
MacLaren:Lintas for criticizing a competitor's ad campaign.

A classic Wayne & Shuster send-up from the late 1970s for Gulf.

An early commercial from the Bank of Montreal's "We're Paying Attention" campaign. A tough-talking cabbie dreams of saving Air Miles for a vacation getaway, courtesy of Bank of Montreal.

A representative commercial for McDonald's.
A charming and sentimental Christmas scene with Sam and Sarah.

A typical Vickers & Benson billboard for McDonald's,
this one promoting a special offer on McChicken and Filet-O-Fish.

# The World Is Your Oyster

MasterCard Travellers Cheques
Travel With Confidence

**Bank of Montreal**
We're Paying Attention

One of a series of ads showing that even a bank
can have a sense of humour.

One of the last
commercials done
for Ford before
the carmaker fired
Vickers & Benson
in 1987 after
thirty-one years.

# THE SIGNS OF THE MULRONEY/CAMPBELL TIMES.

"Over the last five years the restrictive economic policies
of the Mulroney/Campbell Conservatives have put
1.6 million Canadians out of work. And caused
over 300,000 bankruptcies.
How many more lost jobs will it take for the Tories
to realize that deficit reduction *must* be balanced
with job creation."

This is a paid political message by the Liberal Party of Canada.

A Liberal Party ad from the 1993 federal election. The theme of the
campaign was "jobs, jobs, jobs." The windows plastered with
going-out-of-business signs were meant to graphically show the devastating
effects on employment wrought during the Mulroney era.

Still from an ominous anti-smoking commercial Vickers & Benson
created in 1993 for the Ontario Ministry of Health.

**Because you didn't wait
for her to mention it.**

An award-winning
poster for
Amstel Beer.

Scenes from a series of commercials to launch Molson Breweries'
Signature Series of beer. Each commercial equated the skill of
craftsmen to the quality of the product.

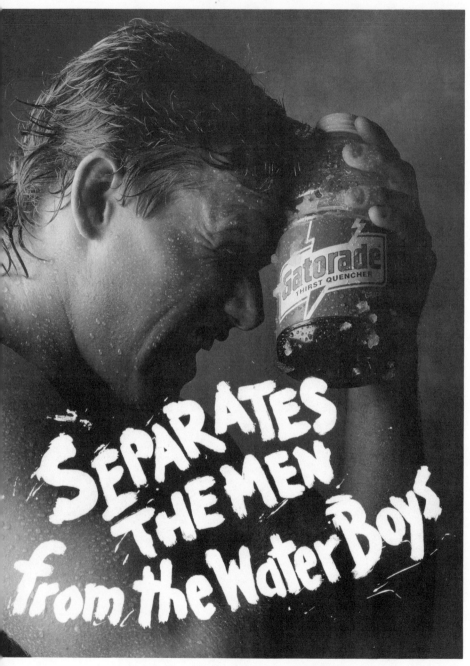

Vickers & Benson boosted sales for Gatorade with a series of
provocative posters featuring sweaty athletes.

Stills from two commercials Vickers & Benson created to pitch the Shoppers Drug Mart account. A beautiful blonde looks for make-up tips. The feisty grandmotherly type lives independently in the country, and depends on her pharmacist for support.

"We Can Help" was the slogan. The pitch failed.

# THE BULLS.
# THE JAZZ.

# BIG SCREEN.
# LARGE PIZZA.

One of a series of "Heineken haiku" posters created by the agency in 1993.

# CHAPTER 5

ONE WEEK AFTER blasting his colleagues for failing to agree on an action plan for Vickers & Benson, Hayter summoned the managers to the executive boardroom on the fifth floor.

In one corner of the room stood a magnificent Inuit sculpture of a polar bear on a marble pillar. In another was a multimedia mix of TV monitors, a VCR and overhead projector.

Philp, Satterthwaite, Bell, McCormick and O'Malley took seats around the enormous leather- and glass-topped oval table. Joining them was Joe Warwick, the head of the promotional department.

There was none of their usual kibitzing. The men sat transfixed, the air leaden with expectation.

Hayter stood at an easel, drawing a diagram with circles and arrows. In the centre of the circle he wrote CREATIVE POWERHOUSE.

He put the marker down and began talking.

"As everyone knows," he started slowly, carefully choosing his words, "whatever we do today is not going to be static. It's going to be moving, it's going to be flexible. So this is a beginning, it is not the end. And it really is, quite frankly, a small beginning. But I think it's an important beginning.

"We spent a lot of time talking about a creative powerhouse, and we tried to define it. I think we got caught up in our underwear. The reality is if we are going to be here in a big way at the end of this century we better be a creative powerhouse. Because what separates us from our clients is our ability to generate those ideas that make a difference for them in their businesses. And that's what they buy. If they don't get them from us or our competitors they're going to go elsewhere.

"And there are already things happening that are unravelling the traditional agency business. Media buying has broken away and has been doing so on an increasing basis over the past several years and we're now starting to see it with the creative product. One of the major, major global brands, if not the most famous brand of brands in the world, is now going outside their agency of forty or fifty years to find creative solutions."

Hayter didn't have to mention the brand by name, because everyone knew the one he meant. Coca-Cola Co. in the United States had bypassed McCann-Erickson Advertising, its long-time New York agency of record, to hire Creative Artists Agency, a talent company run by Hollywood legend Michael Ovitz, to prepare the bulk of its 1993 ad campaign.

The move stunned advertising agencies on both sides of the border. The fact that such a prestigious brand was being plucked from its rightful place on Madison Avenue and given to an *arriviste*—from Hollywood no less!—caused widespread consternation verging on panic.

The *Economist* had an astute explanation for Coca-Cola's unprecedented move.

"Mr. Ovitz is indeed a predatory businessman, happy to operate on turf far away from his comfortable patch," the magazine reported. "But though CAA and other talent brokers may dip into advertising in future, the Coke incursion is a symptom of deeper problems in the ad industry.

"Increasingly, clients are unhappy with their advertising and their agencies. Many agree that creative standards are sinking: just try to name a truly memorable commercial less than five years old. If that does not change, ad agencies will be ever more vulnerable to upstart rivals."

It was a warning designed to make even the coolest brows in Adland break out in a sweat. Certainly, the management team at Vickers & Benson took the threat extremely seriously.

"We as an industry are challenged," Hayter continued. "I don't really care about them. I care about us, and what we're going to do to compete. We talked a lot about how we organize and the kinds of businesses we should be in. And we got hung up on it. We got hung up on it because it comes very close to home. Each and every one of us has established their role in this company and a degree of comfort. And each and every one of us has defended those roles very strongly.

"I see that as a strength. I see that as something that people believe very strongly in the role they have, the capabilities and skills they bring to this place and the passion they have for both of those. So that is a great strength.

"One of the things we need to do, though, is harness those and really push them as hard as we can while bringing it all together as a team. So organizational structure cannot be set aside while we pursue the individual 'centres of excellence.' We have to have centres of excellence, but we have to have a way to bring it all together so that we can be one powerful communications company. Because there isn't going to be any single front that's going to win for us.

"Every front has to be terrific, every front has to be able to make a difference. It is the combination of those that is going to make a big difference in the long run. As we all know, the way that our clients are communicating and establishing long-term relationships with their customers is multifaceted. It isn't just one communications vehicle. So I want to address that.

"And I also want to talk about 'creative powerhouse.' Creative powerhouse can be the work that leaves here and the impression it leaves on people. If it leaves a big impression that leads them to action, that stimulates the growth of our clients' business, that's one way of looking at it.

"But another way is to redefine how we do business. Organizationally, we have to be creative. And so what we set out to do today is a beginning. It may seem very revolutionary. I don't think it is. I think it's maybe revolutionary for this company. It may be revolutionary for several companies. But it's something I believe is necessary. It is something I have thought a lot about. It's not something that just popped up as a solution over the last week.

"But the interaction that we had and the passion that we have for one another's position forced me to say we need to do something fairly dramatic. We just can't go ahead as we are and make small moves. It must be very substantial moves. So I want to give you the reasons why, and then I want you to challenge it. I want you to challenge it and I want you to shoot it down. If you don't shoot it down we're going forward, and we're going to get on with it."

He paused for effect. The others in the room sat stone-faced.

Hayter's tone was unyielding.

"I want us to begin with certain realities," he said. "The reality is that business is starting to break down into centres of excellence as a source for clients to go and buy. And so we have to have certain centres of excellence if we are going to be appealing. We have to be a centre of excellence for advertising. We have to be a centre of excellence for what I call 'the new kind of advertising.'"

By that he meant advertising that strives to make sales happen now, not six months or a year down the road. He cited recent retail-oriented commercials the agency had prepared for McDonald's in Ontario. Commercials that sold the product—whether it be pizza, McRibs or twisted fries—but simultaneously added to the fast-food chain's overall personality, its "share of voice" in the market-place. The cash register rang, yet did so in an engaging, brand-enhancing manner.

There must be more of this "new" kind of hard-working, dual-action advertising, Hayter insisted. "Right through to getting a counter card in a bar for Molson's or a window banner in the Bank of Montreal branches that takes our advertising all the way through right to the teller.

"And so how we structure to do that is important. Do we integrate those or do we segregate those? And I want to talk about that.

"The other thing that we cannot lose sight of is that we deal with certain types of clients. Clients' roles are changing. It used to be the brand manager was the custodian of the brand, and they had a separate sales promotion department. Because they're downsizing they are now beginning to understand integration, and are bringing those functions closer together.

"Advertising, sales promotion and direct marketing are now being handled, in most cases, by the same person. Brand PR is being handled also by that person. Corporate PR, which has to do with financial, community relations and things like that, is being handled outside. And event marketing—which is becoming more and more important because as companies move away from brand and corporate advertising the move towards replacing that with something the corporation stands for in the community is becoming more important.

"And that, too, is being handled by the chief executive office or the marketing department. So we have to be able to deliver those centres of excellence, but we have to be able to connect with the clients as they change. So I want to talk to you about how we do that."

His preamble over, Hayter was ready to get down to specifics. He turned again to the easel with the diagram.

"I see several centres of excellence, and I'm going to start with advertising, because that was our beginning and right now that is still the majority of our business."

Hayter pointed to one of the arrows orbiting the big sphere marked CREATIVE POWERHOUSE. He wrote ADVERTISING beside it.

"We have to have, as a centre of excellence, advertising. And I put here 'advertising' as it's been known and defined in the agency business since the beginning of time, and that is image and corporate advertising.

"What we now have as a company, however, is advertising and then we have the make-it-happen-now advertising in a separate area. It's not integrated, it's segregated. If we are going to become an integrated company with integrated capabilities, the notion of having advertising segregated instead of integrated to me makes absolutely no sense—especially when we consider that our clients are thinking that way.

"Our clients don't sit there and say, 'This is a piece of advertising that accomplishes this, and this is a piece of advertising that's going to get people to come in and buy my product now; I want a different group at the agency to work on it.' They expect the people who work on their business to be able to deliver that.

"We are set up to segregate, and right now segregation may make sense because it is the way we think. We have to change the way we think. We have to have integration. We have to have brand-building, sales-building advertising that goes right through to a counter card or a tray-liner. These are on a continuum. They are not segregated or in separate locations."

So he wrote BRAND-BUILDING and SALES-BUILDING beside the arrow to indicate that both functions should be one and the same.

Beside another arrow he wrote MEDIA. The 1991 merger of Vickers & Benson's in-house media department and Peter Simpson's Media Canada firm had given the agency a "unique strength" in the marketplace, already a true centre of excellence, Hayter said.

By the third arrow he wrote DIRECT to indicate the growing importance of direct-response marketing as yet another centre of excellence a successful agency must cultivate.

By the fourth arrow Hayter wrote PUBLIC RELATIONS. By the fifth he wrote EVENT, referring to sports, community and entertainment activities staged as a soft-sell approach to product promotion.

"We have an opportunity to build a centre of excellence here," Hayter said. "This is something that we do, and we do opportunistically, but we are not focused, we are not committed to this."

Hayter drew a sixth arrow, and labelled it SERVICES to represent the agency staff in administration, accounting and office support.

"Although they don't contribute directly to our creative work, they are very important to us," he said. "We have to have the best people behind us finding new ways to save money, to do things faster and quicker. To give us the technology and research, always probing to find out things that we can do to make our business work more efficiently. We can never leave these people out. They have to believe that they're working for a creative powerhouse."

His diagram complete, Hayter was ready to get down to the nitty-gritty, to spell out how he was going to bring his dream agency alive.

The media function was being ably handled under the Genesis flag, he said. For now, there would be no major changes or reassignments. The advertising department, on the other hand, was to be totally restructured.

"We're going to make a very, very dramatic change," he said. "We're going to team up Terry Bell with Bruce Philp. We're going to remove Bruce from account services. And Bruce is going to become something like—the title is to be determined—creative director.

"And in this role Bruce is going to be responsible for the strategy of our advertising. He is going to be responsible for understanding the workload, the assignment of the work, making sure the work gets done right down to the button. And he's going to make a commitment to that and he's going to make it happen.

"The quality of the work is Terry Bell's responsibility. Terry is going to establish for us the criteria that we believe we need to have in place to be a powerhouse."

Philp and Bell's task would be to ensure the department had the talent and wherewithal to generate big campaign ideas across the advertising continuum, from TV commercials to in-store posters. "Account management," Hayter said, "is going to be reassigned to Jim Satterthwaite and myself."

Direct marketing, meantime, would continue to be headed by McCormick, while Warwick would stay on top of public relations and event marketing. Richard Cousineau, the agency's chief financial officer, would be in charge of the services department.

Hayter turned back to his diagram.

"So what we now have is one, two, three, four, five, six centres of excellence that we are going to sit down and develop individual plans for to determine what we are going to do to make each and every one of those a power. Power in the context of what we want to accomplish as a company.

"We've got to raise the level of our game."

He paused to let that sink in. The others merely studied the diagram on the easel. If they had opinions or objections, they kept them to themselves.

Hayter had one last bombshell to drop.

"If we are going to be a true powerhouse, we have to have the ability for these [centres of excellence] to work together. And to do that we need someone who can tie it all together. Somebody who believes in it passionately. Somebody who understands it. Somebody who can teach it. Somebody who can be the person who drives us to think that way. Because we have to expand our thinking beyond just the centres of excellence.

"So we're going to have someone who connects us all. And that's going to be Terry O'Malley."

There was a small stir in the room as heads turned to see how the living legend, the agency's spiritual father, would take the news. His poker-face didn't flinch.

"Terry O'Malley is going to be the weaver," Hayter continued. "He is going to be the guy who brings us together and makes sure that we build, as we're building our centres of excellence, a power in integration."

His plan revealed, he was ready to sum up and open the meeting to discussion.

"So what we now have is a commitment to excellence in each of the fronts, and we have a commitment to make it happen on integration. We have deployed our capabilities. We have focused our capabilities. We have deployed our people in a way in which they can aim at something,

something they are very good at and something we can deliver on."

The trick, he said, will be to reshape the agency so there is interdependence but no duplication of effort or trampling of egos.

"If we overlap so that we're all bringing something unique to the party we will have a powerhouse that's much bigger. It will give us the kind of commitment to the future that we need. And if we all commit to it, it will not only give us individual passion, but team passion. This is the beginning of something that's going to aim us to be a creative powerhouse.

"I would now like to open it up for comments."

Philp was first to speak.

"The only cautionary note," he said, "is account people will wonder where they fit in."

"Each and every one of us," Hayter answered, "is going to make a commitment right now that this will not leave this room until we all agree to how we're going to market it, package it and communicate it so that people can understand it and don't feel threatened and get excited about it. And that is going to take a lot of thought in management.

"We're not going to run out and do this next week. We need to orchestrate it. We need to think through it, right through every account. We've got to commit to one another that this stays among us.

"To that point Bruce, yeah, there are going to be a lot of people that are going to say, 'Holy shit, I don't get this, therefore, I don't buy this.' And they've got to get it, they've got to understand it.

"As we all know, change threatens almost everyone. And there will be a lot of people threatened by it. The more comfortable we can make them the better, because this will work."

"Account people can look at it another way," Satterthwaite added.

"They can look at this as a way to help them do better advertising for their clients. Here we are organizing their resources, giving them the resources, to deal with that. If we position that in a positive and constructive way they should feel good about it."

"It's a very innovative plan," agreed Warwick.

"As far as events and public relations are concerned, there's a huge commitment necessary to bring them up to code. As far as sales promotion goes, the concern that I see is I think there's a difference between the collateral material that is part of the advertising group and has to flow from it, and what is probably more conventionally known as sales promotion, which are the contests, sweepstakes, couponing programs that really require a special expertise.

"I don't know where that fits in."

"I don't know either," conceded Hayter. "This is a resource that supports these centres of excellence, but it's not a centre of excellence."

"Because there's no money in it," Warwick cut in. There are hundreds of sales-promotion firms in the market-place, and even if there is massive rationalization, the survivors will still have to hustle for every assignment.

"There's not a profit centre there under an agency banner," he cautioned. "To make this whole work, that expertise is going to definitely be required, but maybe on a contract basis."

Bell was up next. "For everybody in the room, it is important to understand that I am really behind this," he said. "I think the whole notion of putting Bruce's thinking-horsepower into the creative department in a partnership relationship to ensure what goes out is the best work we're capable of producing is really a stroke of genius.

"It would be a mistake to minimize the strategic aspect as we've discussed the day-to-day management of the creative department. The day-to-day management is critical. I think that Bruce's management abilities are going to help us a ton in organizing the workflow, and where our needs are in terms of strengthening, from a personnel standpoint, the department. That's a huge job."

Bell was especially excited that O'Malley would be the point man to devise a plan to integrate the various agency functions—"to keep us honest."

"We talk about Gatorade as being a great story. And it is a great story, but we have a whole advertising campaign that we have just done where there's no resemblance to the point-of-purchase material that has just been done.

"And although we're proud of all those dimensions, there is no weave between any of the stuff. Imagine if we're winning now, imagine if we harness all of this into a really fully integrated thing. It would be astonishing!"

McCormick had listened to the exchange with a sullen expression. The others may have warmed to Hayter's proposal, but he would reserve judgment. When it came to his turn to comment, he looked away. "Pass," he said.

He was convinced the plan would profit Bell and Philp, but what was in it for him?

Bell took up the challenge.

"What this allows me to do is spend a great deal more time, one, doing the work and, two, paying attention to the standards," he said. "With or without Bruce we would have reached the conclusion that what this agency needs is a full-time creative director."

Then Philp jumped to the defence.

"Clients want more strategic thinking, fewer Suits," he told McCormick. "This is a pretty neat way of solving that problem."

When O'Malley finally spoke, it was to give Hayter's scheme his blessing.

"I think it's very exciting," he said. But the man who had a mantelpiece full of awards had one proviso.

"There's no award for weaving," he said, a sly smile creeping across his face.

For the first time that morning, laughter rang through the room.

Never one to let a good line go begging, Hayter corrected him. "The weaver of gold," he admonished.

The brief levity did nothing to lift McCormick's dour mood. When Hayter asked if he had changed his mind, the direct marketer again said, "Pass."

Hayter thought it best to let the matter drop for now.

"Well, hopefully we'll knock you off the fence," he said. "Because I want you to be excited about it. What I want is, how might we make this better? Because this is what we're doing. So how do we make it better?"

As it turned out, McCormick never did buy into the scheme. He quit instead, deciding to pull up stakes and move to New York to work as a direct-marketing consultant. Vickers & Benson would be his first client.

His abrupt departure should have come as no surprise. He made no secret of his distaste for Ontario's New Democratic government, or for Toronto's conformity to all things politically correct. He hated the former for its left-leaning policies, the latter for its strict anti-smoking by-law. As a heavy smoker, he was outraged.

McCormick was certainly not the only one hooked at the agency. Bell and Gordon were in the same fix. Chances were if you couldn't find them in their offices, they'd be across the street at Treats, the local coffee bar, notepads in hand, puffing and comparing notes on a new campaign.

"We're grownups, and we're not allowed to work the way we like to work!" McCormick fumed.

"But that's not really the reason I'm leaving. If I wanted to I could ventilate my office. At the end of the day, the real major reason is that I don't want to wake up at seventy-two years old and say 'Michael, you could have gone out on an adventure.'"

At forty-eight, his gut told him it was now or never. "Even if it doesn't work out and I come back, I will not have any regrets when I'm older."

As McCormick was readying to leave the agency and country, Hayter called another executive meeting, this time to to hear a special guest.

David Hurst, a former executive in the steel industry turned management consultant and university lecturer, was to give a report on a study he was making of Vickers & Benson. O'Malley had heard Hurst speak at a seminar and was so impressed he arranged for Hayter to meet him.

Hayter was equally taken with the English-born, South African-raised Hurst. It was decided he should be commissioned to help coach the agency through its rebirth.

Hurst sat at the head of the table, a slide projector at the ready. Gordon sat cross-legged in blue jeans behind him. Ringing the table to Hurst's right were Satterthwaite, Cousineau, Philp and O'Malley. To his left sat Bell, Hayter and Joe Warwick.

And beside Warwick sat Laurene Cihosky from the direct-marketing group. The fact that this petite, dark-haired woman was there at all was extraordinary.

Despite the fact that Vickers & Benson's staff of some 240 people was evenly divided by sex, she was the first woman asked to sit in on one of these bull sessions.

One of those abiding ironies of the advertising business is that women, the target of so many sales pitches, have been all but shut out of the senior ranks of the agencies that create the ads in the first place.

For the most part, they were relegated to the secretarial, administrative and media departments. That began changing in the 1980s as bright young women, flush with MBAs and marketing degrees, began knocking on more and more agency doors. Growing numbers of them gained admission.

None, however, had yet made it into the coveted corner offices of Vickers & Benson, a firm steeped in the culture of strutting masculinity. While other agencies around town were filling executive posts with women—and one, Saatchi & Saatchi, had promoted its top female executive, Liz Torlée, into the president's chair—the glass ceiling at V&B was shatter-proof.

In no small measure, the reason was the jock orientation of the men who controlled the firm. O'Malley was a fanatical sports enthusiast, as was Hayter. They looked at business like a game of baseball or football to be won or lost by the calibre of the players and the intensity of the competition.

Their speech was riddled with the metaphors of the athletic world. There was talk of being part of the team, of going the distance, of scoring goals. O'Malley, whose office was plastered with sports memorabilia, was never far from the sports pages. Hayter had a framed picture of Willie Mays in a place of honour on his wall.

Corridor chit-chat was about last night's game, or which horse looked good in today's race. It was the kind of manly, locker-room environment many women found intimidating and exclusionary.

All the most senior positions in the agency and its affiliated enterprises were held by men. And yet some women did buck the odds to wangle their way into the boys' club. One was Carole Rivard-Lacroix, vice-president of Vickers & Benson's small Montreal service bureau. Another was Mitty Turnbull, the senior executive on the Gatorade account. But when it came to making the big decisions, the "guys" always closed ranks.

Cihosky, however, looked to be a contender for membership to the club. But it was only by accident that her nomination was being considered at all. If fate had twisted another way and McCormick had opted to stay, she would still be on the outside looking in.

"This is work in progess," Hayter told the assembled group. "David has been in and has probably interviewed everyone in this room except for Laurene. David is going to talk to us about some of the things that he has learned.

"We're aimed at becoming the creative powerhouse, a power source with multidimensional business units—centres of excellence. We're really moving towards that target. There are many barriers that David has uncovered that need to be resolved so that we may hit those targets from the day we announce it. We have to have the right culture, the right structure and the right rhythm in the way we interact.

"When we met on the first occasion, one of the things we talked about was one of the biggest problems we have is coming together as a team. These barriers that we're talking about are being addressed so that when we do go, we go as one, we all know where we're aimed at, we all know exactly what everyone is supposed to do and the mission is clear.

"When you put it all together, it is one powerful movement for us."

One of the barriers Hurst had run into was senior management's obsession with secrecy. Hayter and O'Malley would have to change their ways if everyone was to be able to share in the decision-making process. They grudgingly agreed.

"It doesn't rest on one or two or three people's shoulders," Hayter admitted. "It's not to say that you people have been resisting it. We just haven't included you in it. So it's important that we all understand so that we all come up with solutions."

With that, he asked Cousineau to divulge the agency's finances. It was an exceptional invitation, given the firm's private, and tight-lipped, ownership.

Feeling awkward in the spotlight, Cousineau began fumbling with an overhead projector, finally slipping a transparency into place. But just as he was about to reveal the company's financial position, he knocked the projector to the floor, breaking the bulb. Turning crimson, he said he'd have to find another machine.

He left with snickers circling the room. "I knew I should have got an easel," Hayter deadpanned to O'Malley. They both laughed like schoolboys. When he caught his breath, Hayter explained the joke to the others.

Earlier that day, he had in fact tried to rustle up an easel for the meeting. But the agency only had two, and both were in use. When he told O'Malley, the agency chairman quipped: "How many easels does it take to change the culture of an organization?" Hayter guessed the punchline: "The answer appears to be three."

The room exploded with guffaws.

Cousineau reported back that it would take some time to get a replacement, so Hurst took over and began his portion of the show. He explained that what he was about to give them was the same presentation O'Malley had seen. He clicked on his slide projector.

In professorial tones, he began his lecture about management change as it pertains to two different kinds of organizations, those that are oriented to hunting, and those to herding.

He used the analogy of the bushmen of the Kalahari Desert, who for thousands of years eked out a spartan but comfortable living hunting and foraging. It was only within the past twenty or thirty years that they began herding and farming on the borders of the Kalahari, with devastating results. The fabric of the once close-knit society began fraying at the seams.

"If we could understand how hunters change, if we could understand how hunters become herders, we could probably understand how entrepreneurs become bureaucrats," Hurst said.

The others in the darkened room slumped in their chairs, exchanging sideways glances. It was not at all clear how a lesson in anthropology could be the least bit relevant to Vickers & Benson.

Unperturbed, Hurst continued his lesson.

There was no hierarchy in the desert, he said. It was a highly egalitarian society where people were skilled at a multitude of tasks. Leadership was transitory. The "workday" was only three or four hours, leaving plenty of time for the men to talk about game, and the women to gossip about the social comings and goings.

"There are no secrets in this organization," Hurst explained. "This is, of course, what gives them the ability to be leaderless, because everybody knows the mythology and everybody knows just what to do."

But when the bushmen began settling the land, this easy way of life was transformed. They built permanent settlements and corrals for their animals. That led inevitably to the formation of hierarchies, assigned roles and rigid ways of doing things.

"They could no longer reach consensus about what to do. They got into endless fighting. The incidence of alcoholism, violence, murder have gone up out of all proportion, rather like North American inner cities," Hurst said, pausing to let that sink in.

His "students" merely shuffled in their seats.

"They can't reach decisions and consensus any more and one of the reasons, of course, is they've stopped talking to each other," Hurst said as he advanced the next travelogue slide. "As soon as each could aspire to have their own possessions they didn't want to share them with anybody else."

Nor is it a phenomenon unique to the bushmen, he said.

"It struck me this was the story of our lives. There are indeed two modes of living. We have the hunting mode of living, which is open, based on intimacy, sharing and situational leadership. Then you have the herding mode of existence, which is closed, in the sense that you just can't come and join any herding community the way you could with a hunting community. It's built on privacy rather than intimacy. It's built around possessions and the accumulation of possessions. It leads to hierarchical leadership."

If the bushmen's society is falling apart, it is because they no longer have a shared mythology, a common set of values, Hurst said. There are obvious lessons for the corporate world.

Hunters are egalitarian. There is constant breaking up and formation of teams to mix and match skills depending on the tasks at hand. There is an immediate return—that day's kill—and feedback about what hunting techniques worked. By necessity, each member of the tribe must be multi-talented, because each is mutually dependent on his neighbour.

In contrast, there is the herding system, with static, stratified structures, a delayed return on investment, highly specialized jobs and individual conformity.

Inevitably, young companies, much like hunting societies, turn into herders over time, Hurst said.

Companies are founded with ad hoc teams, whose players "disperse quickly and can change composition quickly so that you can get the right composition of the team players. The information which is shared in this young organization is going to travel on networks. Everybody knows everybody's business. Everybody knows everybody's personal aspirations and fears. There will be no secrets, no confidentialities. It is total open communication."

Recognition, not money, is the glue holding the group together, Hurst lectured. Click. Another slide.

"Recognition that you have the opportunity that you've got. It's recognition of each other's contribution. It is a psychic reward. These are the most exciting, nerve-wracking times of your life, working in a young organization.

"All these elements interact to form a system. Communication tends to be open and unshielded. A condition of trust, you might say, develops in this organization, where you tell the truth and don't get killed for having done so.

"A sense of shared purpose, or mission, that transcends the individual tends to emerge. A mission is not a strategy. It is a winding road to an over-the-horizon goal.

"With this articulation of mission the organization comes alive. It now has a life which transcends the individuals within it. You try some things, they work, you try doing some other things and they don't work. You can start to build cause-and-effect relationships as soon as you start taking action."

Eventually, patterns emerge of what does and doesn't work.

"Those bundles of action that do work you put into a package and you name it 'strategy.' With the articulation of strategy you can now crystallize the rest of the organization. Those roles which were so flexible and were chosen by the individual participants can no longer be left that way because you now have a strategy which requires jobs to be done, and they have to be repeated on a regular basis. So your roles become tasks. Job descriptions. Standard operating procedures.

"Those teams which you could form so loosely now have to be more permanent, because you've got a job you want repeated day in and day out. You need a structure, you need some hierarchy. Those networks which were so dense and thick and everybody knew everything that was happening—you can't afford those any more. You know what you want to measure. You know you ought to look for deviations from plans. You're going to put in systems. Accounting systems, data processing systems."

At this point, money, not psychic rewards, becomes the motivation. The transition from hunters to herders is complete.

"It's about this stage that the living animal starts to die, because the founders have made a bundle of money, the place has gone public, they've got a whole lot of options they didn't have before, they're a bit bored with the routine they've created, it's not as exciting as it was before, so they leave.

"People are now totally replaceable. You can now hire a president. You can hire a CEO. And the organization has become a bit more of a mechanism."

There was a slow dawning of understanding in the room. Hurst's anthropological analogy was finally starting to make sense. He was no longer giving them a boring *National Geographic* tour. In his oblique way, he was talking about Vickers & Benson. About them.

"There are two types of organizations," Hurst resumed. "One is the learning organization, which is our hunters. Receptive, resilient, adaptable, creative. The other, of course, is the herders—the hunters that made good. And in the process of making good for the very best of reasons they became rigid rather than receptive, they became stable rather than resilient, they became controlled rather than creative, they rely on repetition rather than experiments. You want to do the same thing over and over again. And, of course, they get totally focused on results.

"And you say to yourself, 'Shouldn't there be a symbiotic relationship between learning and performance? Can you not learn and perform?' And you should be able to.

"You have the learning organization which develops the strategy which feeds into or creates the performance organization which executes the strategy. And what you need is a feedback mechanism into the learning organization and away you go, around and around, getting better and better, continuous improvements.

"Unfortunately, it doesn't work that way. And one of the major problems is, of course, success. In a boom, like we had in '83 to '89, everything seems to work. Almost everything you try works. So the result is there's no feedback. It's as if you write exams for six or seven years, each year you get advanced into the next grade, but you never get an exam back with an answer. And, of course, you develop a considerable amount of hubris."

And when boom turns to bust, as it did in the early nineties?

"Nothing works on the strategy side, and you get feedback on everything that you did during the last six or seven years. All the answers come back. All the marks. And shit, you've forgotten the question! And so what you have is a total short circuit of the learning mechanism in the organization. The long-delayed feedback between action and result is the worst possible condition for learning."

As Hurst talked on, heads began nodding in agreement. He was describing Vickers & Benson to a T.

Hurst returned to his desert metaphor to drive home the point.

"In hunting, you learned fast, because there was fast feedback. But the learning organization has long since been destroyed by the performance organization, because herders kill hunters if they find them on their land. Shoot them down on sight. And so what we have is our classic boom/bust relationship, between performance where everyone looks like a genius—then bust, everyone looks like idiots."

In a panic, staff are fired, companies teeter on the edge of bankruptcy.

After painting this doomsday scenario, Hurst posed the question everyone was anxious to hear.

"The question is, what do we do about it?"

There is a way to convert herders back to hunters, he promised, but it entails a considerable amount of attitudinal and structural adjustment.

"You've got to change the way people interact socially if you want to reinvent the business. You've got to get them back into the hunting mode of interaction to come up with a new technical system that's going to create the next herding generation. Open boundaries—you've got to break down the walls between departments."

Bingo! But how do you do that?

"You can't just go back to the desert," Hurst said, advancing the slide projector. "There are clients out there with existing business, and we have to eat in the meantime. So there's a great problem of how do you reinvent the organization whilst keeping it safe."

Naturally, Hurst had a theory about that too. This time, he borrowed an ecological analogy. There were inward groans. Please, the mood in the room shouted, get to the point! But Hurst was not to be rushed. He still had another carousel of slides.

"It helps to think of an organization as a forest," he began again in his roundabout way. "Forests go through a cycle. In the beginning, there was the seedling, which was in an open patch that got sun and rain."

Fast-growing trees tend to colonize the open patches, and over a period of time certain trees do better than others. They grow tall and shade their competitors. Eventually, they mature into a forest.

"But these forests are curiously vulnerable, because they are all of the same species, all roughly the same age. It makes them vulnerable to catastrophy. It turns out not only are they vulnerable, but it is essential that they do get exposed to catastrophy, because the only way to renew this forest is to take it through a process of creative destruction."

There were a few bemused smiles at that.

"Essentially, what you have to do is burn the forest in order to create open patches in which new organisms can come and go through their exploitation phase. So we have a cycle here."

He showed a slide with a diagram of an ecocycle.

"The first solid line is your classic life cycle. Birth, growth, maturity, decline and then creative destruction, renewal, exploitation and back again. So your forest has got to be a patchwork of organisms at different stages of their development. You always want to have some open patches where it's been burned. You always want to have some that are being colonized. You want to have some that are conservative and producing results, if you will.

"And you've got to have some that are going through a stage of turmoil. You don't want to do all of the forest all at once because it tends to screw things up."

Vickers & Benson no doubt had its own share of patches, he said as a joking aside. "Probably too many on fire at the moment." But the bottom line "is that in order to renew you have to destroy in some kind of creative way."

"Many young businesses starting off get their impetus from the high growth rate of the markets they're in. In the personal computer market, at one stage there was an enormously high growth rate. A lot of businesses could play pioneer opportunists who could not survive unless there was a high growth rate.

"You certainly see it in the advertising business. In booms, you will see a whole lot of pioneers, opportunists coming in to set up their boutiques. There are many more spin-offs where you've got people going out on their own to a high growth-rate opportunity. Effectively it's an open patch, equal access to sun and water, and everybody can exist. Then the business matures, and you get into the conservation phase. That's the ad business today. You're looking at consolidation. You certainly see that worldwide in the advertising industry."

But just like the mature forest that must go through a period of renewal brought about by fire, so must an industry, and the companies within it, go through a stage of crisis and fluctuation.

But out of that there will be a phase of mobilization, marked by creative tensions which then lead back to the exploitation, or pioneer, phase. And so the cycle starts over again.

In the early 1970s, Vickers & Benson was propelled along by the tremendous growth in the Canadian economy, he said. "But then towards the end of the eighties you have the conservation phase and there was consolidation taking place. We're in, I suspect, the back loop between creative destruction and mobilization. It's at this stage, in phase four mobilization, that you first start to have a sense of control of your destiny.

"V&B is coming out of creative destruction. This is a generalization. You've still got businesses which are in the conservation phase; you have some which are still exploiting."

To complete the cycle and to experience regrowth, it is necessary to have tension when you are in the mobilization stage, he explained.

"Tension is essential. And as you know, in my interviews with you I kept on looking for the tensions, the pulls. Because those are the sources of energy. They can be sources of negative energy or they can be sources of creative energy. What we have to do is find out how to make them creative."

This academic chatter was wearing ever thinner. Hurst was beginning to lose his audience. Where's the good stuff on Vickers & Benson? Hurst picked up his pace.

"The vision and the values are important steps of tension," he said as he skipped to the next slide. "You can't go forward to a future that is totally different from the past. But you can't go forward with all the values of the past. You can't carry your possessions with you. But what you can take with you is the mythology.

"So the vision and the values are tensions. You have to have competition within the organization, but you have make sure that it stays in the ballpark. That you don't have fights breaking out amongst the fans or in the streets."

He clicked to a slide of Toronto's SkyDome stadium.

"And if you can have your vision and values like the shared dome of co-operation, then your arena becomes a cauldron."

The goal, he said, must be to encourage intra-agency tension, but only within the self-contained confines of the larger corporate structure. Otherwise, anarchy rules.

"What we have to do in the mobilization phase of pulling this organization together is to develop the shared vision and values—which is what we can buy into—as the crucible, the container that holds us together. And then we can compete like crazy inside.

"How is this achieved organizationally? On the one hand you have to have your performance organization in place."

From what he had gleaned so far, this was not the case at Vickers & Benson.

"One of the feedbacks I got in the interviews was that you spend a lot of your time trying to get things to happen that should be routine, that you shouldn't have to worry about; things that should schedule themselves, things that should appear on time without you having to expedite.

"Your performance structure and operations have to be in place. There have to be rules and they're going to be hierarchical."

It doesn't have to be a stifling bureaucrary, but there must be a system and a set way of doing things, he said.

Next, there must be "hunting" teams weaving across the tapestry of the organization that could, say, ferret out new business. Once the contract has been bagged, the routines that have already been put in place to service accounts would kick in.

Vickers & Benson is not yet capable of accomplishing this, Hurst sermonized.

"We haven't got the performance layer down and that means that we can't play the hunting roles that you'd really like to play."

The solution?

"You're going to have to break down the barriers. You've got floors that are separated. You've got functions that are separated. There's going to have to be a lot more moving in and out. We cannot make it alone in this business. We need each other. It's also a mutual acceptance of each other's competence. And an egalitarian society of less layers, less hierarchy, less bureaucracy."

Vickers & Benson, he concluded to evident relief, must create the right "micro-climate for learning. We're looking at sharing the burden, at getting much more openness and accessibility to numbers and results. And a good deal more fission and fusion in the organizational structure to get the right players together in the hunting bands."

Hurst was still troubled by the deep divisions he had uncovered while doing his staff interviews.

On the one side were the old guard who thought of Vickers & Benson in terms of one big family. That meant a willingness to co-operate for the greater good of the organization. They shared a feeling of ownership in the company, of teamwork in getting the job done.

On the other were what Hurst labelled the "new breed," the recent recruits who talked of competition, going it alone, instituting a star system for top achievers and re-creating the agency into a creative hotshop.

"It was very clear coming out of the interviews that there are very different sets of values," Hurst told the group. "What we can't have is these being seen as opposites.

"If we have no co-operation, we just have arrogant prima donnas. If we have no competition, we have faceless grey people. What we're looking for is some kind of synergy."

There are too many ambiguities caused by differing visions and values held by those who want the Vickers & Benson "family" and those who were bucking for change.

The split manifested itself in even the most fundamental areas, including a disagreement over what "creativity" meant. To some it was the coming together of disparate disciplines into one interlocking whole. These were the "frame makers." To others it was the pursuit of breakthrough ideas that smashed convention. They were the "frame breakers."

"Tension," he reminded them, "is a source of energy, both positive and negative. It can destroy us, and it can make us successful."

And it is up to the agency's leaders to chart the way, something that must be done before the forest can renew itself, before the hunters can re-emerge.

"One of the clear lackings was that you have senior people who don't know the overall situation, don't know their own particular situation and cannot be held accountable for results. John and Terry were carrying the entire burden of all the problems.

"They were taking action that other people could see but they couldn't interpret because they didn't have the framework. Just going through the numbers today is a very small beginning to that.

"We need process. We've got to get people talking to each other."

No disagreement there.

"I've been herding," Hayter said, voicing the consensus sentiment. "I want to be a hunter."

With that admonition, Hurst turned the floor over to Cousineau, who by this time had another overhead projector set to go. Hayter cautioned the room that, as a private company, the figures they were about to hear were classified and strictly confidential.

Cousineau had sombre news to report. In the years since 1991, when Hayter, Satterthwaite and Bell joined the firm, revenues had shrunk alarmingly. The drop was easy to pinpoint. Since 1991, the agency had lost significant clients from both the government and private sectors, the national McDonald's account being the largest.

The forecast for 1993 was glum, Cousineau warned the group.

"I've been doing this job for about fifteen years now, and quite frankly I've never seen revenue erosion so quick, so early, and so substantial in those fifteen years. This is an industry phenomenon. It ain't just us."

Many of the agency's divisions, including those devoted to production, direct marketing and healthcare marketing, were performing acceptably.

The area that was most worrisome was advertising. The lack of sub-stantial new business to balance the across-the-board cuts from existing clients was crimping the bottom line.

Exacerbating the situation was the agency's heavy rent and growing payroll.

"We've managed to spend seventy-one cents on the dollar paying our-selves," Cousineau said. "The key right here, ladies and gentlemen, is the salaries. If you're looking at why it's 70 per cent [of total expenses] it's because our clients aren't paying us what we want to be paid for what we do. The client has more money than we do, and we should be very diligent in trying to get the best deal for the best product."

Gatorade was a case in point. Vickers & Benson had just received an outstanding performance review, yet the agency was still struggling to make money on the account.

Moving to new quarters should help ease the financial burden, Cousineau said. He calculated the agency would save about $2 million over eight years.

But the fact remained that Vickers & Benson was facing a loss in 1993 after making modest profits in the previous two years. And it didn't look any brighter for 1994.

"If you look at our client base and where the revenue is going to come from in 1994, I can't see any substantial growth in terms of current clients," he said.

"If you guys don't do it here," he added, pointing to the revenue line on a graph, "then sooner or later the Grim Reaper is going to take that salary line, because that's the only place I have to ensure the well-being of the group."

Hayter interrupted to reassure the group there was hope for a turn-around in fortunes.

"We have not incurred bad debt," he said. "We have not borrowed one dime from the banks. We've had extraordinary return on the money on deposit at much higher rates than we had when there was more money flowing through at higher interest rates."

Overhead expenses had been pared. The next step was to improve efficiencies.

"The critical issue is the revenue, and the fair compensation for what we provide, and also taking advantage of the incremental budget opportunities that are out there," he said.

"I like to dream, because I think if you do dream the hunter in you also comes to life."

He confided that the agency was looking to add $5.5 million in revenue if it could successfully land a number of assignments currently on the street. There was a catalogue assignment worth $700,000 up for grabs, not to mention the fact that Shoppers Drug Mart was casting about for a new agency, and Vickers & Benson had a good chance of landing the business. A win would add $3 million.

And if the Liberals romped back to power in the next federal election? It could mean revenue of more than $1.5 million in new contracts from Ottawa if the agency played its cards right.

"The opportunities are mammoth," Hayter said. "And I like to dream. I like to go for it."

Hayter's pep talk helped smooth some of the worry lines of the executives grappling with the scope of their firm's wobbly financial picture. At least now they knew just how serious the situation truly was.

That, of course, had been Hurst's intention all along. If everyone knew how big the pot was, perhaps they'd play better cards. But that didn't mean the game would get any easier.

# CHAPTER 6

I F THE LIFEBLOOD of an agency is its roster of paying clients, anyone
could see that Vickers & Benson was in desperate need of a transfu-
sion. Hayter certainly could. The day he became president and chief
executive, he was already thirsty for a fresh supply.

Even as he was negotiating with O'Malley and Bremner to join the
agency, one of the firm's biggest clients, the Woolco department store
chain, was walking its account, worth revenue of $900,000, out the
door. At the same time, the Ontario tourism account, worth $2.2 mil-
lion, was also preparing to leave. There were indications that 3M
Canada Inc. was getting ready to bolt.

Within a month of his arrival McDonald's announced a review of its
national assignment. Vickers & Benson lost big—to the tune of another
$1.6 million in lost revenue.

Hayter was stunned by the carnage. "I'm sitting there with $4.7 mil-
lion in the hole," he despaired.

He had little choice but to go after new business. There were cuts he could make in staff and overhead, but there was no way he could cut deep enough to make up for the shortfall.

So the veteran campaigner, who had participated in perhaps one hundred new-business battles over his career, led a frantic hunt for blood, chasing everything up for grabs. The strategy paid off, at least initially. In short order the agency's coffers were enriched by some $2 million. But it was, at best, a catch-as-catch-can operation. The agency's search for a revenue injection was motivated by necessity, but not necessarily clear strategic thinking.

Hayter explained it this way: "Discipline is very hard to practise in new business pursuits. You try to have a disciplined approach to it, but then you hear something moving and you say, 'Gee, I don't know. We just heard that this account is getting a little soft. Revenue is off, and we need to fill it in. Otherwise, we're going to have to cut bodies or dump some overhead.' So you're often looking at new business for the wrong reasons.

"If you develop a strategic approach to new business, it requires tremendous discipline to live by it. Because it's hard to turn down the opportunity to have volume coming through in terms of dollars. This, like any other business, is a business. You have to be able to meet your nut.

"Too often new business is a pursuit of things that really don't fit with you. If you stopped and thought about it, you wouldn't chase them. It's sort of like that sexy woman, or that great big hunk: 'Gee, that looks pretty good.' What you see isn't always what you get. It's true in new business."

In Vickers & Benson's case, however, it was hard to be disciplined, at least it was when Hayter appeared on the scene.

"We had a company with no defined vision or goal. The decade was coming to a halt. The company was being sold. New management was coming in. Bill Bremner was no longer in charge. What are we going to be? People were looking for a focus."

And there was Hayter and his new management team trying to get a fix on Vickers & Benson's coddling code of values, one that encouraged senior staff, known as "uncles" and "aunts," to routinely cover for their colleagues' flubs. The rapacious everyone-for-themselves mindset belonged elsewhere, in other agencies. At Vickers & Benson it was all family.

Hayter knew he couldn't just march in and trample such ingrained loyalty. In fact, he wanted to foster it. But he also needed to effect change at a time of utter revenue chaos.

So he fretted and schemed and rushed headlong into a pursuit of new business. The only problem was that as some clients came in the front door, others, feeling neglected, escaped out the back.

Hayter figured he knew exactly why.

"I learned a long time ago that the best new business you have is the business you already have. And while we were going after the new business to make up for the business that had gone before we got here, we weren't establishing the kinds of relationships with our existing clients that we should have. We weren't working with them towards building their opportunities. And their opportunities are our opportunities.

"At the end of 1991, which was eleven months into my first year, I wrote a January note to the staff, saying here are our goals for 1992. The first one was we're going to nail down every client we have. We're going to build their relationships, gain their respect and trust, and grow their businesses. And the second was we will go after those new business opportunities that we feel are right for us."

In other words, Vickers & Benson would quit chasing ambulances. It would also stop pitching assignments that just didn't fit naturally with the agency. The Ontario Lottery Corporation was a prime example of the latter.

Lottery officials had determined they could get a better bang for its buck if each agency on its roster, including Vickers & Benson, competed in a bidding war each time a new project came up. It was a radical concept for an industry used to a winner-gets-all mentality.

Hayter hated it. He felt it mitigated against everything he held to be true about the relationship between a client and an agency. The ideal arrangement, he believed, was built on shared commitment, on a sense of partnership developed over time. How could that happen if the agency was in a state of constant review?

"I'm sorry," he concluded. "You're not going to get the kind of commitment you need to do the best work. We all know that continued rejection is less of a motivator than repetitive successes. That formula of shoot-outs on projects is something that just creates a negative environment. So we wanted to get out of it."

And that's exactly what happened. Vickers & Benson quit taking chances on the Lottery, gambling the odds were less risky with clients that saw things Hayter's way.

"Even though it cost us money, we decided we did not believe that was the best way to create advertising."

Agency management redoubled efforts to work with its clients, to cement relationships and thereby gain more business from them. The strategy began to bear fruit. Additional assignments were being added to the agency's docket.

Vickers & Benson already had Quaker Oats' pet foods division. Then it added Life and Cap'n Crunch breakfast cereals, granola bars and Gatorade. When McDonald's introduced pizza to its menu in 1992, V&B

helped with the Ontario launch. A few ads to promote the Bank of Montreal's sponsorship of show-jumping competitions led to the big-budget "We're Paying Attention" campaign.

Popular TV and outdoor ads for Amstel beer convinced Molson Breweries to give the agency work on other brands, including the imported Heineken and Corona brands. Gradually, the agency was infiltrating Molson's mainstream advertising.

Repairing a frayed connection with 3M Canada also had the potential for bringing big gains to the agency. When Hayter arrived, Vickers & Benson's relationship with Bruce Moorhouse, the head advertising executive with 3M, was at an all-time low.

"In fact, we could have been let go," Hayter said. "Jim Satterthwaite and account director Bob Nunn worked very hard at earning his trust and respect, and buying the time to demonstrate that we valued him as a client. Whatever was wrong, we would put right. And we did do that."

Growing with existing clients allowed an agency to be more selective about seeking prospects. That wasn't always so important. When times were good, agencies like Vickers & Benson could afford the extra staff to pursue new accounts. But those days were gone. The fat had been trimmed, forcing stripped-down management teams to steal time from existing clients.

Clients always caught on eventually. Service began to slide, in some cases to such an extent that they went looking for an agency that would pay the kind of attention their dollars should command.

"That's no way to build the business," Hayter conceded. "That's certainly not the way we're going to do it. I think we've been very good the last two years in retaining and building [existing clients], and opportunistically adding [new ones]."

Some companies will go after anything that moves. Hayter prefers the studied approach adopted by the thriving Toronto unit of Chicago-based Leo Burnett Company Ltd. "They grew and grew with the best of the best."

Indeed, many of Leo Burnett's clients go back decades with the agency, including Kellogg's and Pillsbury (1952), Procter & Gamble (1958), Allstate (1957) and Maytag (1965), using such household icons as the Jolly Green Giant and Tony the Tiger. As their clients grew, Leo Burnett grew with them.

Like Vickers & Benson, the agency was privately held. It was a client-focused company, one that continued to believe in such "old-fashioned" ideas as developing and training its own talent base. It recruited promising young account executives on university and college campuses, a practice few other agencies still follow.

The results paid off. In 1988, the Toronto operation was billing $101 million and had a staff of 162. By 1992, billings were up to $153 million, and the staff complement had risen to 188.

"When they do go after new business, they go after new business that fits," Hayter said admiringly.

It was a model that he wanted to emulate, so he established two rules that would help Vickers & Benson get there:

1. An agency is known for the companies it keeps. Work with the clients you have, help them grow and the opportunities for additional work will present themselves.

2. Have a hit list of potential clients, and work diligently to cultivate relationships in preparation for the day they decide to look for a new agency supplier.

There is a third rule he didn't mention: Be prepared for the unexpected. Occasionally, an account goes begging because there has been a change of management, and the newcomers suspect they can get better service elsewhere. More commonly, it is simply a case of a client deciding to test the waters to see what marketing solutions another agency might recommend. And oftentimes a client just wants to keep its agency on its toes, to underscore that the relationship should not be taken for granted.

If an advertiser does cast its net, and it is a large assignment, interested agencies must be ready to put their names in the hat on short notice.

Such was the case in the summer of 1993, when Shoppers Drug Mart, Canada's largest drugstore chain with seven hundred outlets from coast to coast and annual sales of $3.2 billion, decided it was time to review its $20-million ad account. It had been held by one agency, Kert Advertising Ltd. of Toronto, for twenty-seven years.

Management at Shoppers quite rightly guessed that its advertising was due for an overhaul. TV spots, starring the husband-and-wife team of Michael Tucker and Jill Eikenberry from "L.A. Law," had grown tired and limp. Typical ads would show the pair cavorting in a store aisle, flirting over greeting cards, cosmetics or prescription drugs. She was cast as the self-assured woman of today; he the dim but likeable hubby.

The campaign was ridiculed by other agencies as being ineptly executed and too cute by half. By comparison, Kert's previous ads starring Beatrice Arthur of "Maude" and "Golden Girls" fame seemed wittier, fresher and more daring. Arthur's trademark double-takes and snappy one-liners had been masterfully exploited for comic effect.

Kert Advertising would have stayed with Arthur, but after six years in the role of corporate spokeswoman, she had decided not to renew her contract. Eikenberry and Tucker seemed like the logical successors. Their TV series was a hit with viewers, and twosomes—such as the coupling of James Garner and Mariette Hartley for Polaroid cameras—had proved popular in the past.

There were other reasons why Shoppers wanted to explore agency alternatives. The chain was under attack on two fronts. First, there was new competition from mail-order prescription services offering cut-rate dispensing fees. Second, the Ontario government was proposing to out-law cigarette sales in pharmacies. Both developments had the potential to seriously undermine Shoppers' revenue base. Management decided urgent action on the marketing front was needed to forestall further sales erosion.

When word hit the street that Shoppers was looking, a predictable feeding frenzy ensued. Seldom did an account of this size and prestige become available, and every agency that felt capable of taking it on was anxious to be in on it. Hayter figured Vickers & Benson had as good a chance as any of them.

Along with seventeen other agencies, it submitted a reel of work to showcase its creative prowess. Hayter was astounded when Vickers & Benson did not make the short list of contenders. There were five, all based in Toronto, that did: The incumbent, Kert Advertising; Chiat/Day Inc.; Doner Schur Peppler Inc.; Ogilvy & Mather Advertising; and J. Walter Thompson Co. Ltd.

J. Walter Thompson later withdrew when Shoppers launched a pri-vate-label cola which would compete with one of Thompson's core accounts, Pepsi-Cola.

"We were already beginning, in anticipation that we would make the list, to work on it," Hayter said. "And when we didn't get it, we were just absolutely devastated. We just felt cheated. Not cheated so much. I felt it was wrong."

He soon found out why the agency was snubbed.

"I think it was really a big error in judgment on my part," he said. "We did a video. The video spent a lot of time talking about philosophy, and how we do business."

It ran fifteen minutes, and included testimonials from McDonald's and the Bank of Montreal. It profiled Vickers & Benson's media capabilities, and featured clips from some of the agency's best commercials.

Where Hayter miscalculated was not providing Shoppers with what it wanted at this stage of review. Management only wanted to see the work the agency had done for its clients. That is what the other agencies fighting for a chance to make the list did.

"Your client testimonials were terrific," Stan Thomas, Shoppers' executive senior vice-president of marketing, told Hayter when he pushed for an explanation. "We were looking for that in the next phase. You hurt yourself."

That smarted, and Hayter shouldered the blame. But how was he to know? "Usually they want to know more than commercials."

His judgment call had been wrong, but Hayter wasn't ready to give up just yet. He decided there was only one recourse—appeal to Thomas directly.

It was a tactic that had worked for him in the past. When he was managing director of Alberto-Culver in England, he was dumbfounded to discover the Woolworth chain, which was one of his biggest customers in Canada, did not carry one of his company's products in its stores. Hayter was determined to change that.

After numerous attempts to book an appointment with Woolworth executives failed, he went to their offices to see if he could wrangle a meeting. He arrived at 7:30 in the morning, and sent a message up to the president's office asking for five minutes of his time. A message came back saying he couldn't see him. Undaunted, Hayter wrote another note asking for two minutes. It was 10:30, and he said he would wait in the lobby until the office closed if need be. There was no response.

At 2:00, he sent another message saying he was still there.

About 3:30, a secretary finally came down to say he would get his meeting, but not that day. Hayter would have to call back in a month's time. That meeting did take place, and Hayter convinced Woolworth to stock Alberto-Culver products.

"After two or three years, they were one of our biggest accounts," he liked to boast.

Would the same gambit work with Shoppers? Hayter felt he had nothing to lose. He had examined, and rejected, all other options.

When Vickers & Benson failed to make the list of contenders, the agency staged a powwow to discuss what to do next. Someone suggested that one member of the staff, TV producer Tessa Waisglas, should put in a good word. After all, she was a close friend of Shoppers chairman and chief executive officer David Bloom's daughter.

"Absolutely not," Hayter declared. "That's not the way to go. What respect would he have for me and this company if we went in through an employee?"

Well then, someone else said, why not pull a few strings and get a friend of Shoppers founder Murray Koffler to recommend Vickers & Benson? Bloom was Koffler's protégé, and would listen to his counsel.

Hayter nixed that plan as well. "That's using influence," he said.

There was only one answer for it. He would plead the agency's case with Stan Thomas.

As he had done with Woolworth, he arrived at Shoppers' headquarters at 7:30 in the morning. He called Thomas's office from his car phone. He wasn't in. He tried again and again. At 8:40 he finally connected with Thomas's secretary. She said he was due in shortly before 9:00, but had to go immediately into a meeting.

"Okay. I will wait in the lobby," he told her. "I just need a minute with him. If he can do it, tell him I'd really appreciate it."

That worked. The secretary said Thomas would grant him his minute. He met Hayter in the lobby and took him for a cup of coffee.

As it turned out, Hayter got twenty minutes. But the news was not good. No, Vickers & Benson could not be on the short list, Thomas told him. The Shoppers selection team had already agreed to limit it to four agencies, and felt even four was pushing it.

"I'm sorry," Thomas said.

Hayter was not deterred. "I don't want to sound pushy," he said, sounding just that. "I could very quickly piss you off because you're trying to tell me 'no' and you want me to go away. How about this. All I ask of you is to give me the same assignment you give everybody else. You don't have to spend any time with us.

"All you have to do is give us a two-hour presentation. I promise you, Stan. We will blow you away. That's a promise. You will not be let down. That two hours will be every bit worth your while. You've got nothing to lose, and you've got one hell of a lot to gain."

"How can I turn that down?" Thomas replied. "That's a very powerful story."

Hayter tore back to the agency, feverish with excitement. He told the rest of the pitch team that it was a go. Bell and Gordon were designated to prepare the creative work under Philp's guidance, marking his debut as the agency's new director of creative services. Meantime, Bruce Claassen, president of Genesis Media, the agency's planning and buying partner, began crunching numbers and co-ordinating media alternatives.

They worked at a frenetic pace. They had been granted one last chance to convince Shoppers that Vickers & Benson deserved a place on the candidate list. If they blew it, they blew it forever. The presentation was to take place one week before the "real" finalists were to make

their pitches, and that meant long hours of hashing strategies and film-
ing two commercials to demonstrate the agency's creative approach.

On the appointed Monday morning, the V&Bers met with Thomas,
senior vice-president of advertising Gord Stromberg and Neil Everett,
the research director.

"They were very understanding, because we had worked entirely in a
vacuum," Hayter said. "So they were forgiving. But we impressed them."

Vickers & Benson won the round. The agency would get to strut its
stuff before the full Shoppers selection committee. But that was only
ten days away, and there was still much work to do.

A couple of days later, Everett met with the agency to offer some additional information that could be used to fine-tune the presentation.

"So we made some changes," Hayter said. "It was pretty hard to
change it dramatically. Our strategy, in our opinion, was bang on. Our
insights were right. We felt our work was right. Executionally, there
were some things that we didn't have right. Those we could change, we
did."

A lot was riding on winning. The agency needed the account for the
revenue it represented but, almost as important, it was a test of Hayter's
grand scheme to rebuild the firm around the "creative powerhouse"
concept. It was the first time the management team would pitch under
its new configuration and corporate mandate. If they could pull this off,
it would bode well for the future.

Secrecy was of the utmost importance. Since no announcements had
yet been made to the staff about structural and executive changes,
Hayter and the rest of his team played their cards close to their vests.
Certainly, there would be no leaks from Shoppers. The wholly owned
unit of Montreal-based giant Imasco Ltd. remained Velcro-lipped, only
supplying the most basic of information when the trade press came

snooping for details of the review.

In fact, in all the stories leading up to the final pitches, Shoppers officials never once confirmed that Vickers & Benson was even under consideration.

The week of the presentations, *Marketing* published a story about the review, which included a picture of a smiling Norm Kert, chairman and chief executive of the incumbent agency.

"Some are calling it the stealth review of '93," the magazine reported. "It's one of the biggest agency competitions to date this year, but has received little [media] attention...Incredibly, it's also the first time in almost twenty years Shoppers has reviewed its business. The last time, in early 1976, Shoppers gave half the business, representing the western provinces, to McKim Advertising. A year later, Kert won it all back."

The account meant "more than just billings and bodies," the article stated.

"Emotionally, for me it's such a major part of my business career," it quoted Kert. Shoppers became his first client in March 1966, one month after he opened for business in Toronto.

"The emotional aspect of not working with Shoppers is important to me," he said. "Naturally, we're doing everything we can to retain it."

Kert's strategic platform had three planks. The first was to recognize that the agency was up against stiff competition from much larger multinationals. Second, it would keep Eikenberry and Tucker. Third, there would be a new take on the creative execution.

*Marketing* quoted only one other player willing to go on the record. Ira Matathia, president of Chiat/Day, said his agency was "charging after [Shoppers] with all we've got."

"The challenge is to prove that we've got the answer for them," he added.

His comments, innocuous though they were, resulted in Matathia getting his wrists slapped by media-shy Shoppers. The other agencies prudently refused comment.

When *Strategy* contacted Jim Satterthwaite to see if Vickers & Benson was on the short list, he answered no. At that point, that was technically true. Shoppers had not officially listed them.

And so Vickers & Benson entered the race, no one the wiser.

The days leading up to the presentation were a whirlwind of activitity, as one would expect of a pitch of this scope.

"New business has got the highest highs and the lowest lows," Hayter said. "The greatest low is when you have given it all [and still lose]. Everything is condensed in a very short period of time. You have to learn, in a new business situation, what it could take you a year in another situation.

"You are expected to understand the consumer and the relationship that consumer has with a product or service so that you can gain insights that will allow you to differentiate that product or service from another one. You have to develop a strategy, and often execute that strategy in terms of creative, media and integrated marketing. Often you don't sleep."

That was certainly the case with Shoppers.

"Every night you'll wake up and you'll think about it. That's true of any major advertising project you're working on, but because this has a beginning and an end in a short period, it just forces your involvement, to the point where you get so emotionally involved. And when that phone call comes and they say, 'I'm sorry,' you just crash."

But there was no time for worrying about losing now. The team was too busy tinkering with the final details of the pitch. They went over

and over their presentation, honing it down to two hours. There would
be no gimmicks, no clever banter. Just the straight goods. Two finished
commercials were edited for airing. Several other storyboards of proposed spots were drawn and ready.

Hayter was satisfied. "Unquestionably, it was the best new-business
experience I've had since I've been here. It was a small core group, all
on the same page and committed. We were able to focus, agree and
challenge. The tension was positive tension."

In a normal working situation, there is the opportunity to confer, to
sleep on decisions, to tread softly around egos. But in the rush of a
pitch, there is seldom that luxury of time for social niceties. Opinions
are blurted out under the pressure of looming deadlines, and to hell
with the feelings of colleagues.

"You tough it out. But at the end of it, there's a lot of raw nerves, and
sometimes injuries. In this case, we didn't have that."

Philp, in particular, shone in his new role as director of creative services. He took an immediate liking to his new role, although he still felt
a bit awkward. The fact that clients and the rest of the staff had yet to be
officially told of his new status made his task that much harder. He
found he had to tiptoe, when marching purposefully was more in keeping with his style.

"Obviously, there were lots of old habits that had to be broken," he
said. "You know, interjections that you just had to catch yourself from
making because it wouldn't be natural for someone in that position."

But the masquerade held, and on the appointed Thursday afternoon,
he and the rest of the pitch team were as prepared as they would ever
be. Everyone felt right about what they were about to present.
Confidence was high. Philp drove the team over to Shoppers' headquarters in his van. On board were Hayter, Bell, Gordon and Claassen.

All were aware of the challenge in front of them. The competitors were formidable, and each had good reason to want to win.

One of Chiat/Day's key clients was Canadian Airlines, whose prospects at that time were clouded, with speculation rife that a final showdown with Air Canada was imminent. Having another big client like Shoppers on its roster would provide comforting security to the agency, the country's eighteenth largest ad firm.

Doner Schur Peppler, ranked nineteenth in size, was an experienced retail agency, with an impressive track record of award-winning campaigns for Canadian Tire Corporation and Leon's Furniture. But those were clients of long standing. The agency could certainly use the boost that winning Shoppers would provide.

Ditto for Ogilvy & Mather, one of the most respected names in advertising. Although it counted such heavyweights as Campbell Soup Co. Ltd., American Express, Joseph E. Seagram & Sons, Unilever Canada Ltd. and Chesebrough-Pond's (Canada) Inc. on its client roster, Ogilvy, ranked sixth in Canada, needed a revenue hike to support its expansive empire.

Each of them had already pitched their cases by the time the Vickers & Benson team was up to bat. They were second last to present, a good place to be. But the incumbent drew perhaps the best lot as the final presenters.

Kert, ranked twenty-ninth in agency size, was also the smallest of the agencies in the contest. Shoppers was its bedrock account, so losing would surely mean big layoffs. In every respect, it was fighting for its life.

"It would be very easy to write Kert off," Hayter reminded his colleagues. "The fact of the matter is, Kert has been with them for twenty-seven years. A lot of history, a lot of success. From a few stores to seven hundred stores. I do not rule them out."

With those thoughts racing through their minds, the Vickers & Benson team pulled into the parking lot. The tension was high. Everyone knew what was at stake, that their small group represented the hopes and aspirations of the entire agency.

They met the Shoppers review committee in a large presentation room. In attendance were Bloom, Thomas, Stromberg and Everett. Shoppers president Herb Binder was also there, as was Arthur Konviser, senior vice-president of public affairs. Other executives, representing the chain's cosmetics and private-label divisions, bumped up the client contingent to ten.

It fell to Hayter to open the session. He said there were three objectives they wanted to accomplish that afternoon. The first, convince Shoppers' management that Vickers & Benson was the best agency to be their partner. Second, demonstrate that V&B could deliver superior advertising. Third, show the agency was so in sync with Shoppers that the relationship would endure for many years.

Then, just as they had rehearsed it, he unveiled a large rectangular board. In one corner was the Shoppers logo, in another Vickers & Benson's signature. In the middle of the board were three circles, arranged like a shooting target. The circles were blank.

The Shoppers people stared at the board, eyebrows cocked.

They're all looking at me thinking I'm nuts, Hayter thought to himself. Not to worry. They'll catch on. He raised a marker to the board and pointed to the innermost circle.

"Great work starts here," he said, "with the insight." He wrote the word inside the circle. "What is it that you have in your product or service that really, truly differentiates you from your competitors? If you have that, then there is the possibility you can have great advertising. If you don't have that, you will never have great advertising.

"The insight allows you to develop strategy. Bruce Philp is going to present the insight and the strategy. From great insight and strategy, you can develop breakthrough creative."

Hayter then introduced Gordon and Bell, and said they would present the advertising that flowed from the insight and strategy. Their work formed the second ring of the target, which Hayter marked CREATIVE.

Then he introduced Claassen, designated to talk about Genesis Media's plans to put the advertising to work in the market-place. Hayter wrote MEDIA in the last ring, and drew arrows that shot out from the target's perimeter. These, he said, were meant to represent the different forms of communication that could be supplied by Vickers & Benson's various marketing divisions.

Before turning over the floor, Hayter announced that Philp was no longer director of client services, the position he had in previous meetings with the Shoppers' executives. Now he was head of creative, and that entailed an explanation.

"You're going to see a lot of advertising and creative today," he said. "Bruce did not write one piece of that, even though he is our director of creative services. But Bruce wrote a lot. Bruce wrote the creative strategy that is the starting point of great work. That's what he does as director of creative services. He gets the insight, and crafts it into powerful strategy.

"So when Larry and Terry work with it, they've got something magical, not something where they say, 'What in the hell do I do with this blob.'"

Philp, he said, turning to his favourite baseball metaphor, was a manager, like the Blue Jays' Cito Gaston. "He's the guy thinking, manoeuvring. Now, Terry used to have this job. And he hated it."

THE
*CREATIVE*
EDGE

The solution was for Bell to revert to what he excels at, Hayter said.
And that was writing.

"In my opinion, he's the best. You'll decide that later on. He's a writer
by craft. We do not want Terry managing and doing administrivia. We
want Terry hitting the long ball and knocking in runs."

With that, it was Philp's turn in the hotseat. Shoppers, he said, pioneered the drugstore chain concept in Canada and had prospered for
many years. But the competition had finally caught up, to the point
where Shoppers was no longer unique. Others also carried a wide variety of merchandise. Supermarkets also stocked private-label products.

The solution was to remind consumers that Shoppers was in the helping business. Help for when they were really sick and required prescription medicines. Help for when they had the sniffles and needed
something to feel better. Or help with beauty aids when they just wanted to look their best.

With that build-up, he unveiled the campaign theme: "We Can Help."

The slogan prompted an ambiguous reaction from the Shoppers'
people. A murmur of "umms" and "ahs" and "interestings" went around
the room.

It was up to Bell and Gordon to convince them the line was right for
them.

They started by describing two commercials in "storyboard" form—a
series of TV panels sketched in comic-book fashion. Then they showed
how the commercials would actually look on TV. They plugged in a cas-
sette and the first spot came on.

It opened with a superimposed line of copy: "How can we help,
Mary?"

Then Mary, a folksy, grandmotherly type who lived on a farm, came
on screen. Her friends worried about her living alone in the country,

she said, but she liked it.

Quick edits of idyllic farmyard with chickens and cows and the like.

Besides, she added, as long as there was a Shoppers druggist nearby looking out for her blood pressure, everything would be okay.

"We Can Help," flashed the end super.

Next up, a variation on the theme, this time about cosmetics.

"How can we help, Susan?" the super asked.

Susan, a thirtysomething blonde, responded: "I don't want to look like Cindy Crawford." Pause. "Maybe a little."

She likes her eyes, she said, flirting with the camera.

"If eyes are the windows to the soul, I want picture windows."

"We Can Help," the end super reassured her.

Then the creative team showed how the theme could be extended over any number of executions. Seven more storyboards were presented. After that, they read some radio commercials.

The Shoppers executives liked what they saw and heard. "It's terrific," one said. "Great," added another.

Basking in the warm reception, Bell and Gordon gave over to Claassen.

He delivered a consummate performance. He showed how Genesis's clout could generate numerous media opportunities to add value to Shoppers' promotional programs. Genesis was setting up a new division, called Media Entertainment International, to seek out special programming appropriate for its clients to sponsor.

This new division might even produce programming to suit an advertiser's needs, in much the same way that detergent companies used soap operas to hawk their wares. The opportunities for a company like Shoppers, independently or in co-operation with other sponsors, to do the same thing were manifold.

Again, an approving response from Shoppers. The presentation was going well. It was up to Hayter to bring the show home.

He gave a synopsis of Vickers & Benson's breadth of capabilities, mentioning its expertise in public relations, sales promotion and direct marketing.

This was met with a wave of interest. Heads nodded, and notes were scribbled on pads.

Hayter made one last, passionate appeal to say that Vickers & Benson was the right agency with the best solutions.

Then it was over. Hayter thanked them for their attention, and sat down. The room erupted in applause. As they clapped, the Shoppers' executives went around the room, shaking hands and congratulating the agency team for the calibre of their work.

It looked as though Vickers & Benson had a new client.

Afterwards, driving back to the office in Philp's van, the men rehashed the afternoon. They felt invigorated, knowing they had given it their best shot. The presentation had gone eighty minutes over the allotted time because there had been so many questions, such good dialogue. The Shoppers' people seemed keenly interested in what they had had to say. If at first there was some skepticism over the "We Can Help" positioning line, the resistance appeared to melt as the meeting wore on.

The V&Bers felt good. They were convinced the strategy was right, and the creative and media executions were spot on.

"It went just about as well as anybody had any right to expect," Philp said. "I think we did a lot with what little we had to work with. And everybody presented very well I thought."

What made this presentation a joy, Hayter added, was the fact the strategy was so single-minded. Other presentations often contained several ideas, each with different themes that had numerous applications for direct marketing, public relations, merchandising and so on.

"But this was simple. We had one idea based on what we thought was a breakthrough insight."

And the team was loose. There had been minimum stress. "Everything we presented we were able to back up to the best of our abilities. There was nothing there that we could not defend."

But would Vickers & Benson win the prize? That was the $20-million question at the back of everyone's mind.

"I think we've got a real good shot," Hayter concluded. "I also know that the other people will have given it everything they've got."

Philp pulled into the Vickers & Benson parking lot. He and Bell had to dash to a Molson focus-group session. Claassen went home. Hayter worked until 7:00, then took in a performance of *The Phantom of the Opera.*

And waited for the phone to ring, dreading what the news would bring.

The following Monday, Hayter was speeding west along the Queen Elizabeth Way towards Oakville when he barely escaped smashing his car into a transport truck. It would not be his only close call that morning, in more ways than one.

Anxious though he was to find out if Shoppers had made its decision, he had already committed himself to attending a tournament hosted by Cantel, one of his clients, at the Glen Abbey golf course. But to ensure he could be reached in case advertising chief Stromberg called, he rented a pager. It was the first time he had done so and, being a novice user, was a bit flummoxed when the silent vibrator went off in his pocket. He hadn't expected an answer so soon.

He took it out and read the message to call Stromberg. Two phone numbers were listed. He returned the pager to his pocket and called the first number from his car phone, only to get Stromberg's voice mail. He fumbled with the pager again, and began punching the second number.

He was paying more attention to the phone than the road. Almost too late he looked up to see that he was only inches from swerving into the side of the truck. Still rattled, he pulled off the QEW at the exit to the golf course. As he approached the parking lot, he connected with Stromberg.

The two men exchanged opening pleasantries.

"Gord," Hayter finally asked, "is this one of those phone calls I want to receive, or don't want to receive?"

Pause. "It's one you don't want to receive, John."

Hayter groaned, realizing that meant Vickers & Benson was shut out. He was crestfallen. The long hours and high hopes were for naught. The Shoppers account would go to another agency.

Stromberg told him that a winner had not yet been determined, that it would take at least another week to make the final decision. It was down to Kert Advertising, the incumbent agency, and one other shop, he said. He didn't specify which one, but Hayter suspected it was Chiat/Day. That meant that Ogilvy & Mather and Doner Schur Peppler had also been eliminated.

Hayter asked why Vickers & Benson failed to make the grade. Stromberg answered that the review committee really didn't like the agency's "We Can Help" theme line.

Hayter was doubly disappointed. He had assumed the Shoppers people had warmed to the slogan after the pitch team had argued passionately and, it was thought, persuasively for it.

Hayter knew that the agency hadn't made its reasoning clear enough. "We Can Help" wasn't meant to be an indispensable component of the campaign. If Shoppers didn't like it, a substitute could have been written. What was important was the thinking behind the line, not the line itself.

The point of the campaign was to glorify the customer and her relationship with Shoppers, to reinforce the notion that the drugstore was there to help with the right combination of products and service.

Unfortunately for Vickers & Benson, it looked as though Shoppers wanted a campaign to glorify itself—to make the store, not its customers, the hero.

The agency should have spent more time in the presentation convincing Shoppers otherwise, Hayter realized then. After all, Vickers & Benson had done twenty-two one-on-one interviews with consumers to test the line, and it came out on top.

After three decades in the business, there were certain things he had developed a gut feel for. And having seen the research results, even though they were strictly qualitative, he knew the positioning had been nailed, that it was right for Shoppers. There were elements of the commercials that needed some tinkering, sure. Hayter could live with that. But the strategy itself was sound.

However, Shoppers would have had to be prepared to buy into the concept, and it was apparent they wanted something less risky. Hayter assumed they wanted to be challenged, not comforted. And that was probably Vickers & Benson's biggest error.

Hayter put a brave face on his hurt and wished Stromberg and Shoppers well. The call over, and still replaying the conversation in his mind, he suddenly realized he was late for the tournament. The other golfers were already driving away in shuttle carts to the links. As he was backing up to park, he barely missed hitting one of the carts. The startled riders tumbled on to the grass.

Red-faced, Hayter slammed on the brakes. All eyes looked accusingly at him as he leapt out of the car to make sure everyone was okay. He could see this was not going to be his day.

To top it off, he had to pretend he was happy to be there, to hide his disappointment under a mask of back-slapping conviviality.

He took time out to call the office to let the others know the bad news. Unfortunately, there was no time to get together to commiserate. Hayter had to go to a banquet after the tournament, and the next day's schedule was already crammed with engagements.

Work was heating up on the upcoming election campaign, other presentations were on the docket and there was the everyday business of all the rest of the agency's clients to attend to.

The time for mourning would have to wait.

# CHAPTER 7

AYTER WAS RIGHT to suspect that the race for the Shoppers account came down to Kert Advertising and Chiat/Day. The selection committee was torn between the two agencies. In fact, it took two months for them to decide which one deserved the nod. Ultimately, Chiat/Day prevailed.

The ever-secretive Shoppers organization kept the rationale for dumping Kert after twenty-seven years to itself. Stromberg, in a one-page press release cloaked in marketing mumbo-jumbo, only hinted at the reason.

"Chiat/Day presented us with a comprehensive communications strategy and the most exciting and imaginative campaign that would suit our needs for the balance of this decade," he said about his new agency.

When the Shoppers verdict came down, Hayter was already neck-deep in the forthcoming election. There was no time for looking back.

He knew there was a lot of work to be done. Liberal leader Jean Chrétien's popularity was half that of Kim Campbell, who had spent the summer criss-crossing the country in a calculated attempt to show a more accessible, populist side to her personality. There she was dancing the twist in Ontario, kissing babies in British Columbia, talking tough on crime in Alberta.

She put on a masterful performance, and the media ate it up. Her press coverage was decidedly more favourable than critical, and she consistently outflanked Chrétien and NDP leader Audrey McLaughlin at every turn.

Despite the glowing reviews, there was an undercurrent of restiveness, and bitterness, after nine years of Brian Mulroney. Voters were looking for answers to high unemployment. They were demanding a leader who could pull the country from the quagmire of a lingering recession.

It fell to a team of Liberal-minded advertising professionals, including a contingent of top executives from Vickers & Benson, to ensure voters would think of their man when they were ready to cast their ballots.

Vickers & Benson's connection to the Liberal party has roots shooting back to the 1960s. The Grits under Lester Pearson were in power, and that meant their advertising friends were fat with the bounty of government largesse. Chief among the beneficiaries was MacLaren Advertising, which had prepared the ads that helped put Pearson in office.

MacLaren had won the plum political assignment after Louis St. Laurent lost the 1957 election to John Diefenbaker. The agency that had created St. Laurent's ill-fated campaign was Cockfield Brown. Once one of Canada's largest ad firms, it went bankrupt in 1983.

The management of Vickers & Benson in the '60s under then-president Bryan Vaughan felt left out of the game. They, too, wanted a slice of the government's ad pie, and began pestering Ottawa for contracts.

Some work did flow V&B's way, but the lion's share continued to land in MacLaren's lap.

The 1972 election began turning the tide in Vickers & Benson's favour. MacLaren had devised a campaign around the slogan "The Land Is Strong," which was strongly derided as propagandist by critics who saw little strength in a country then mired in recession. The gaffe certainly hurt Pierre Trudeau, who only four years earlier had ridden a manic wave of popularity, who barely hung on to a minority government.

By the next election in 1974, it was evident a fresh approach was needed. Senator Keith Davey was called in to form a new campaign team. He envisioned it to be a consortium of Liberal-aligned agencies, which would pool the talents of their best strategists and creative people.

He christened the group Red Leaf Communications, and one of the charter agencies was Vickers & Benson.

"This new company," Davey explained in his 1986 memoir, *The Rainmaker,* "purposely structured for the campaign, would be a non-profit organization, although some of the participating agencies might eventually do government advertising. I would be the chairman of Red Leaf, which would be headed on a day-to-day basis by [Toronto lawyer and now Senator] Jerry Grafstein."

Other key members who were recruited in the 1974 and subsequent elections included such Toronto advertising notables as Jerry Goodis; Hank Karpus, head of Ronalds-Reynolds; and Tony Miller, president of MacLaren. O'Malley was one of the star recruits from Vickers & Benson.

The agencies agreed to share their expertise in exchange for an eventual payoff if the Liberals won. Davey defended the patronage, decried by critics as the worst form of pork-barrelling, as appropriate and aboveboard.

He was a great supporter of the indigenous advertising industry, and felt Ottawa was obligated to support Canadian-owned agencies at the expense of multinational firms. He decreed there would be "absolutely zero American advertising."

He remains unapologetic for his partisanship.

"I don't have any trouble with it," he said in a 1992 interview. "I think governments, of necessity, are going to advertise. By the very nature of what governments do, there will be a lot of advertising. And I don't think there is any reason why that advertising shouldn't be with some of our friends who have worked hard for us—providing the agency is a qualified, professional agency.

"I remember way back in the Pearson years in Quebec there was a French Canadian organizer [who wanted all the advertising for Quebec]. I thought it was outrageous because he wasn't qualified."

And so to the victors went the spoils, and with the prospect of winning portions of Ottawa's huge ad assignment—by 1992, it had grown to be the largest in the land—there was no shortage of agency volunteers.

The operation of Red Leaf was relatively uncomplicated. Davey and other party strategists would devise a party platform, then brief the agency executives on what was to be communicated in the advertising. Tasks were split depending on the particular strengths of the team members.

Davey was particularly smitten with O'Malley, whose political advertising he described as being "the best there is." O'Malley was given the pivotal job of masterminding the Liberals' television campaign.

Although the Red Leaf team was comprised of executives from a number of rival agencies, there was a surprising amount of goodwill and co-operation. There were exceptions, of course. O'Malley and Goodis, in particular, collided with often explosive results.

O'Malley would complain to Davey that the iconoclastic Goodis was driving him crazy. Goodis, who became Canada's best-known adman in the 1970s and 1980s in no small part due to his political connections, would return the fire with equal velocity.

In his 1991 autobiography, *Good!s—Shaking the Canadian Advertising Tree* (Fitzhenry & Whiteside), he complained that "Keith [Davey] thought Terry O'Malley was the Moses of Canadian copywriting. I never agreed with that. In the first place, Moses was an account executive, not a copywriter. Secondly, like a number of the ten commandments Moses brought down from the mountain, I thought Terry often had a tendency to overwrite, both in headlines and in copy.

"On the other hand, I had great respect for the intuitive skills of Hank Karpus and George Elliott, with whom I was later to work at MacLaren. While their styles were different from mine, we were more closely attuned. Therefore, sometimes I had to bite my tongue when Terry made a presentation.

"It wasn't that the ideas weren't discussed openly. What I had to learn was to be more judicious in my comments."

Goodis's comments enraged O'Malley when the book was published and excerpts of their behind-the-scenes skirmishes were featured prominently in the trade press. He briefly considered firing off a letter of rebuttal but thought better of it. Let history judge who was more instrumental in getting the Liberals elected, he bristled.

Despite the occasional raw nerves, the ads always got done.

Grafstein recalled the excitement of working with the Red Leaf team in a 1984 interview with *Canadian Business* magazine: "There was a terrific synergy. They were competitors who'd never worked together, and I had to run those guys! They were like stallions."

O'Malley was quoted in the same article praising Grafstein's debut as head of Red Leaf. "We had so much respect for Jerry, our sense of competition went away," he said. "He knew the things that cut and wouldn't cut with the people.

"When I thought up the idea of Joe Clark flipping cards, like a failed magician [for the 1980 campaign], Jerry picked that one out long before anyone else did."

But despite their vaunted solidarity and advertising acumen, Red Leaf was not infallible. Trudeau won his majority in the 1974 election, lost to Clark in 1979 and came back to win once more the following year. It lost again in 1984, giving the team a .500 batting average.

When Trudeau resigned in 1984, so did Davey. The party's new leader, John Turner, had made it abundantly clear he did not want a Trudeau loyalist on his team. But a fumbling start to the fall election convinced him to bring in The Rainmaker to try and work his magic one more time.

"With three out of eight weeks to go in the Turner campaign, he called on me," Davey recalled years later. "Well, it was over before it began. I couldn't turn it around."

No ad campaign could counter the publicity nightmare of Turner's infamous bum-patting of prominent Liberal women, nor overcome his unfortunate staccato speaking style.

While Mulroney was in power and Turner was Opposition leader, Davey quit as a backroom strategist, devoting his time instead to being a senator. Then Chrétien decided to re-enter politics.

"I told him very clearly, 'Jean, I'm not going to run your campaign under any circumstances,'" Davey said. "I think he was 60 per cent delighted that I had said that, and I think he was 40 per cent concerned that I was going to walk away from him."

But Davey did agree to help as an adviser to the 1993 campaign, playing a self-described role as "the old man of the mountain." Meantime, by the early months of 1993 the Red Leaf ad machine was already revving its motor.

Grafstein decided to hand over the reins to Kevin Shea, who was then president of the Toronto-based children's cable service YTV Canada Inc. Shea had been involved with the Liberals for twenty years in a number of capacities as a party volunteer, and was a friend and colleague of Grafstein's. But this election was to mark his debut so close to the front lines.

Since he felt he was really starting Red Leaf anew, Shea spent his first two weeks as chairman listening to how the team had operated in past campaigns. Then he spent another two weeks putting together a 1993 version. One of his biggest decisions was to make Vickers & Benson the lead agency, supported with creative and media talent from other shops.

There would also be another Red Leaf, he decided. One made up of theoreticians and strategists. This larger group would comprise officials from the national Liberal office, ethnic groups and representatives from the various regions. Senators Davey and Grafstein were to be among them.

They would be the thinkers offering arm's-length advice to the more public Red Leaf, the one made up of executives commissioned to actually create the ads.

Among this latter group, the key members from Vickers & Benson were O'Malley, Hayter, Bell and Gordon.

Because Genesis Media, Vickers & Benson's media-buying partner, was the government's agency-of-record, it was thought prudent not to involve anyone from the firm. How could it be otherwise when Genesis was buying time and space on behalf of the Tory government in Ottawa?

So an ad hoc media team was recruited. Members included Ron Bremner, a senior vice-president of Vickers & Benson; Shelley Flood, media director with Rubel & Schwab, a unit of Vickers & Benson specializing in pharmaceutical ads; and Shannon Murtagh, chief executive with Toronto's Murtagh Thom Media Inc.

This team would be responsible for the English-language campaign. Another Liberal agency, Montreal's BCP Strategy-Creativity, would handle the French side.

While Red Leaf was being organized, Hayter was adamant that no one from Vickers & Benson should feel coerced into joining. Certainly, there would be no question that O'Malley would take part. Nor was it difficult for Hayter to throw in his hat. But the rest of the staff were free to decide for themselves.

"I just felt there was absolute need for change," Hayter said of his decision to sign on. "I had had enough of an inside position to sense that they really did want to put together a plan that could grow the country.

"I tend to be more Conservative than Liberal in the financial part of my life. But in my heart I'm a Liberal. I believe in what Liberalism stands for. While we do need strong financial leadership, I think it has to be done with a high dose of compassion, that the anger and the fear and the hopes of Canadians are very much up for grabs.

"It does need the kind of government that really does have a sensitivity. I just felt the Liberals, and particularly Chrétien, would bring that dimension."

Hayter gave Shea a list of prospects who might be interested in also joining Red Leaf. Included on that list was Marlene Hore.

The native Montrealer had recently quit the Toronto office of global agency giant J. Walter Thompson after more than twenty years with the company. She got her start in the business as a junior copywriter in Vickers & Benson's Montreal office in 1969. Two years later, she jumped ship to JWT, quickly rising up the ranks to become one the firm's top executives.

She was named group creative director at age thirty, and Montreal creative director two years later. In 1986, she was named vice-chairman of the Toronto office. The following year she attained the singular honour of becoming the first woman to be elected a director of the New York parent company.

Along the way, Hore had worked on a star roster of accounts, including Pepsi-Cola, Dare cookies and Red Rose tea. More recently, she had won acclaim for writing a TV commercial for Choclairs, a chocolate covered biscuit. It featured a table of women swooning over the seductive enticements of a French waiter.

Despite her professional achievements, Hore had been shut out from working on political ads because she happened to work for an American firm. As such, she, and her copywriting abilities, were off-limits to parties looking to recruit top talent for their campaigns. But in 1993, Hore left JWT to devote more time to her other passion, writing screenplays. And when the Red Leaf organizers came knocking, she agreed to help out the cause any way she could.

Hayter recommended that the 1993 edition of Red Leaf be kept lean and mean. Shea agreed. "You can't do creative by committee," he concluded.

Hayter was also insistent that Red Leaf have representatives from other agencies. "V&B is an agency for Canada, not an agency for Liberals," he declared, concerned that too cozy a relationship with the Grits would imperil the agency's chances of wooing contracts from other political parties.

Nor did he think it fair that all Vickers & Benson staff be branded as Liberals.

"I just don't think we have the right to impose upon employees their political preference," he said. "And also, being a pragmatic business person, I want Canada to succeed and I want this agency to be part of it. We can bring a lot. We're one of the largest and most successful and most diverse agencies in terms of talent and capabilities."

Because of its ties to the Liberals, Hayter was convinced the Mulroney government blackballed his company. That was wrong, he believed. "If you're passionate about the country you want to help it, regardless of who's in power."

After all, Vickers & Benson had shown it could work under different administrations. It handled the Jobs Ontario assignment for the New Democratic Party in Ontario, for example. But that was a minor assignment. The NDP had already stripped the far more lucrative tourism account from the agency. Still, it was encouraging that V&B got any work from Queen's Park. At least it showed it could be done.

Unlike O'Malley and Bremner, who always wore their Liberal convictions proudly—and learned to enjoy, or suffer, the consequences—Hayter wanted to play a safer political game. His plan was to move Vickers & Benson to a more neutral position. If any agency staff wanted to work for other parties, they would have his okay.

"I think the best should represent the country, and if the Liberals get in and we're viewed as being an agency that can contribute to the country, we should be able to compete and win. And if it's the Tories, the same thing. Right now, we're not even in play with the Tories. We're labelled Liberal and that's it, even though I know there are people here probably working for the Conservatives," he said.

"So it's time that's put aside. The country is greater than the parties."

Be that as it may, Hayter was prepared to do his damndest to make sure the Liberals won. He stood behind the one-way mirror at focus group sessions to watch as voters looked at and commented on prospective ads.

He even corrected Chrétien's speaking style.

"I said some things that I'm surprised he even accepted. I told him not to wave his arms too much the way he does. To be calm. I said when you're very much under control you're a very powerful persuader. He smiled, but I don't think he appreciated the critique. But I made my point."

Throughout the summer leading up to the election call on September 8, Red Leaf tried on, rejected, refined and explored alternate means to get the Liberal message across.

Red Leaf's first instinct was to paint Campbell as Mulroney in drag. She would be portrayed as standing for all of the unpopular policies the Tories had brought in since 1984.

But the focus groups weren't buying it. The consensus opinion was that slamming Campbell was an unconvincing tactic. It became clear that the people wanted answers, not mud-slinging. They wanted to know what Chrétien would do for them, not how nasty he could be with his rivals.

So Red Leaf shifted gears. It would take more than saying "The Tories brought in free trade, so vote Liberal" to win over voters. The advertising would have to give them solid reasons to vote Liberal. Simply broadcasting the Tories' shortcomings was not going to work.

But as in any election, the window of opportunity was only a few weeks. You had to be ready for any contingency.

"Every day there is a regrouping and new initiatives could be created," Hayter said. "It's all-out war. So the best of plans often have to go out the window. Our position is if we come out too negative it will work against us. We have to come out as professionals and we have to position Jean Chrétien as a leader. Someone who can lead Canada. Someone who has the plan, who has the team and has the leadership qualities to pull it off. That he will make a difference."

At a meeting with Chrétien and his top campaign officials one night in late August, Hayter and other members of Red Leaf debated the merits of the party leader saying "We stand for this…" versus "I stand for this…"

Both Hayter and Bell were strongly in the "I" camp. The focus groups had unequivocally declared they wanted somebody to stand up and be accountable.

"They're looking for someone who's going to lead them," Hayter argued at the meeting. Many around the table felt uncomfortable with the personal focus, wondering if that was really Chrétien's style.

But Hayter wouldn't give up, arguing that "Canadians felt everything was out of control. That their futures are at risk, their security is at risk and they just want someone to stand up and say, 'I know what I'm doing, we've got the plan and we're going to do something about it.' To give them confidence that there is some hope."

"So the 'we' is weaker than the 'I,'" Hayter continued, accentuating the pronouns in the line of copy Bell wrote. " 'I have the plan, I have my team, we will make a difference' is much stronger than 'We have the plan…' The 'we' is too nebulous."

In political campaigning, countless hours are consumed nit-picking over such seeming minutiae. But it is often just these small details that make the difference between winning and losing. Opponents are always looking for signs of weakness. One false move and they pounce.

At another meeting, a debate erupted over the Liberals' platform. There was no question of the thoroughness of the policies. It was just that there might be too many to pin a campaign on.

But one policy stood out from all the others.

"Jobs, jobs, jobs. That's the centre of gravity," Hayter believed. "Own the jobs war, then you can start talking about women's health, crime, education and those other things. But if you go out and you talk jobs one day, this the next day, this the next day, all you are doing is giving your menu.

"If you own 'jobs' as a centre of gravity and keep coming back to that, you will be able, we believe, to control the agenda. And then you can bring out these other points. They will have more meaning."

Hayter also knew the risks of hammering home the jobs issue. The Liberals were talking about building roads and other public works. All would boost employment, but at the taxpayers' expense. That would leave an opening for the Tories, who were pushing fiscal responsibility and debt reduction.

Ultimately, party strategists concluded it would be up to the electorate to decide which party had the winning formula.

"Advertising can only play a small part," Hayter knew. "There are going to be thousands of messages that come at you, from your local newspaper to TV to your local candidate's flyers. And everybody's going to have their shit detectors going, saying 'Which one makes me feel this is a credible plan, and I trust them?'"

As it stood, the pre-writ polls claimed Chrétien held only a slight edge in the trustworthy department, a fact that astounded Hayter, who thought Canadians would have had a much higher regard for the Liberal leader.

"He's Mr. Clean. He's been in politics for thirty years, and there's never been any scandal, or anything remotely close to scandal, around him."

That finding, too, held lessons for the Red Leaf team.

"One of the things we'll be doing is reintroducing him," Hayter said in the countdown before the election call. "Because clearly there's a lot of people who just don't know him. But we're not going to get into character assassination and say he's more trustworthy than she is. There's no reason to believe she's not trustworthy. She's just different."

And if the Tories attack Chrétien's credibility, slagging him as Yesterday's Man? Hayter believed they would pay for that approach dearly.

· "If they come the other way and they do a character assassination on him, it will backfire. Canadians are very fair and generous people. They judge you on what you do, and not necessarily on what you say. If it does come down to direct blows where they cut deeper than they should, then it will backfire," he predicted.

He was right.

While Red Leaf was ready and gunning for the election call, the Tory team was not even assembled. Campbell's party was still scurrying to recruit a consortium of ad executives.

It was to be lead by Tom Scott, a veteran Tory loyalist and former chief executive with Foster Advertising, and Raymond Boucher, president of Montreal agency PNMD/Publitel Inc.

"There are lots and lots of people who have volunteered and, over the next week or so, we'll be filling in some of the boxes on the organization chart," Scott told *The Financial Post.*

"It's organized scrambling. We are not as far advanced, I would guess, as the Liberals are at this point, but it really doesn't concern me."

It should have. Perhaps better organization could have prevented what turned out to be the Tories' biggest ad blunder of the campaign, the infamous TV commercial showing unflattering close-ups of Chrétien's face. "Does this look like a prime minister?" the ad asked. Remarkably, *Maclean's* reported, Scott and party pollster Allan Gregg showed the spot to focus groups without objection.

The ad caused an immediate furore. Kirk Makin said it best in a blistering commentary in *The Globe and Mail:* "With the supposed *crème de la crème* of advertising people and pollsters at their disposal, the Tories have managed to step in every cow flap in the field."

He continued: "The notorious Conservative ad showing Jean Chrétien's face frozen in contorted positions has won hands down as the single most bone-headed act of the election campaign. In 30 seconds of symbolism, the Conservatives seemed to confirm what disaffected voters have been telling anyone who will listen for weeks: Politicians have no scruples. Politicians will do anything to get elected."

Goodis, quoted in *Strategy,* was equally appalled. "It showed contempt for people's intelligence," he said. "Canadians have a sense of fair play, a cultural difference, that makes them recoil at things like this even if they don't like the other person." Campbell, who insisted she had not approved the ad, nor even seen it before it went on air, ordered it pulled. But the damage was already done.

She admitted later, in an article in *The Toronto Star,* that instead of winning votes for her fellow candidates, the commercial did precisely the opposite. "I think the ads cost the seats of a lot of people who would otherwise have withstood a [Liberal] wave," she said.

On October 14, the night the commercial hit the small screen, the Red Leaf team were at Shea's home reviewing the last round of commercials leading up to election day. One of the spots had been filmed just the day before. Like all the commercials Red Leaf had prepared for the campaign, it featured Chrétien talking about issues. This one was about how he promised to be accountable for his promises. He would not change the medicare system, nor tinker with old-age pensions. From his first day as prime minister he would begin the job of putting Canadians back to work and the economy back on kilter.

Another commercial was shot expressly for British Columbia voters, who polls suggested were leaning heavily towards the Reform Party. The spot urged them to vote Liberal so they could have a voice in government, not in Opposition.

Hayter thought the B.C. ad was fine, but hated the other one. It had been a rush job, and it showed. Chrétien's posture was poor, the camera angles not quite right. Neither did it fit in with other commercials already in the can. Chrétien looked like two different people.

"I don't think we should run it," Hayter said. Bell agreed. No sooner had they decided the commercial should be scrapped when the evening news came on with the Tory ad story. The Red Leaf team were dumbfounded. That's the absolutely dumbest thing the Tories could have done, they said.

Ironically, they had earlier toyed with addressing the issue of Chrétien's appearance because research indicated some people would not trust a person who talked out of the side of his mouth. But Red Leaf dropped the idea. That would only be begging for sympathy, they concluded. Besides, Chrétien had long since got over any embarrassment the result of a childhood illness once caused him. Why should ads touting him as prime minister even consider dredging it up? Canadians were bigger than that.

Instead, Red Leaf opted to stick to the high road. Show Chrétien in as prime ministerial a fashion as possible, and keep drilling home the policies detailed in the party handbook, *Creating Opportunity: The Liberal Plan for Canada,* which pundits were quick to dub the Red Book.

"At no time did we assume a majority," Hayter said. "In fact, I think one of the great themes that [campaign chief] John Rae brought to the campaign was under-promise, over-perform. Right to the end we took the position that the majority wasn't there, even though the numbers said they were there. We just kept doing all the right things. We were lucky. I don't think there was anyone that wouldn't admit we had a pretty clean ride. You have to be good to be lucky and lucky to be good, and I think we had that going for us."

Doubtless fortune played a role. But Red Leaf could also credit its own political savvy. Its ads never deviated from the strategy of pushing Chrétien's credibility and statesmanship. And Red Leaf made daring use of its thorough research capabilities.

"All parties use research," noted *Marketing*, "but the Liberals' media research analyzed each riding's characteristics, voting history and other data, right back to Confederation. Ron Bremner, who tackled this along with former Liberal campaign veteran Gordon Ashworth, says the Grits knew their target audience had a larger female skew than the Tories' and was 'less downscale.'

"Because their audience was so varied, they knew they couldn't target it cost-effectively during prime time. So they bought media to have only 60% of the broadcasts during prime time—a strategy Bremner says is unusual for elections. The 40% off-prime media, besides being cheaper, more effectively targeted women, seniors and the un- or under-employed, he says.

"The same flexible approach was used in targetting ethnic groups. In Cambridge, Ont., for example, the Grits ran Portuguese-dubbed radio spots on radio station CIAM. Research showed the local ethnic population stood at 15.4% of the total, which was 15% higher than the national average. Out of the total 18,000 to 19,000 ethnic voters in the area,

37% spoke Portuguese."

The party's private polling, conducted by Insight Canada Research Inc., confirmed the Liberals were on the right track.

In a public-opinion survey done in the week of September 27-October 3, 71 per cent of the respondents said they had seen or heard election advertising. Of these, 73 per cent cited the Liberals, 67 per cent the Tories and 43 per cent the New Democrats. Asked which party had the most interesting ads, 30 per cent said the Liberals, 15 per cent the Conservatives and 9 per cent the NDP, just ahead of the Reform Party at 8 per cent.

The Liberal ads were twice as believable (28 per cent) as the Tory ads (14 per cent), respondents said. Almost the same margin (28 per cent) felt the Liberal ads were more informative than the Tory ads (16 per cent). Only 11 per cent picked the Reform Party. Asked which party's ads made the most sense, 32 per cent said the Liberals, 17 per cent the Tories and 15 per cent the Reform Party. Asked which made the least sense, respondents picked the Tories (23 per cent), NDP (21 per cent), Liberals (10 per cent) and Reform (9 per cent).

Perhaps most heartening for Red Leaf were the scores on the question of which party had the best ads: Liberals (32 per cent), Conservatives (17 per cent), Reform (10 per cent) and NDP (7 per cent). Twice as many said the Tories had worse ads (20 per cent) than the Liberals (10 per cent).

Finally, the all-important question about persuasiveness. Asked which party's ads made the best argument for voting for that party, respondents picked the Liberals (31 per cent), Reform (15 per cent), Tories (12 per cent) and NDP (7 per cent).

Bolstered by their superior poll results, the Red Leaf team gathered on the night of October 25 at the YTV studios to await the verdict of the voters.

"We had a couple of monitors set up and we had a great party," Hayter said. "We celebrated early because it was over so early. At twenty to nine it was called."

The Liberals were on a mammoth sweep that, before the night was over, would take them to a resounding victory with 178 seats. The Tories were all but wiped out, holding only two seats, and the NDP were reduced to eight. It fell to the Reform Party and the Bloc Québécois to duke it out for official Opposition status.

"Everyone was going nuts," Hayter recalled. "We knew we were going to win, but no one could believe the result. I guess there was jubilation, then there was just shock at the collapse of the Tory party. We quickly went from celebration to 'My God…' I don't know why we spent so much time talking about it. I guess because it's a lesson on life. You should never, ever assume you're infallible and invincible. It can happen to any company, any party."

The party began breaking up around 11:00. A small group, including Hayter, took off to a trendy cafe for more drinks. He didn't get home until 4:00 the next morning.

Uppermost in Hayter's mind was the anticipation of a payback for Vickers & Benson's contribution to the Liberal election cause. Publicly, he would only say that he expected his agency to be allowed the chance to bid for federal ad contracts. Privately, he was hungering for the spoils of victory.

"All I know is we're going to be actively pursuing federal government business," he vowed. "Because we are a good agency, I think we will get our share."

# CHAPTER 8

H AYTER KNEW THE time had come to let the rest of the Vickers & Benson staff in on his grand scheme to reshape the agency into a creative powerhouse. But first he had to solve the puzzle of the Terrys.

Neither O'Malley nor Bell was happy. O'Malley because he really didn't relish the idea of becoming a "weaver," the guy who would tie all the agency departments and disciplines—Hayter's vaunted "centres of excellence"—together into a seamless, integrated whole. It sounded too much like a make-work project, and he didn't want any part of that at this stage in his career.

And Bell wasn't keen to become the arbiter of quality for the creative department, as Hayter had proposed. The job description sounded too fuzzy. Besides, people would wonder who really ran the department, Bell or Philp. Wouldn't that just perpetuate the awkward situation that arose when he and O'Malley carved up fiefdoms?

It dawned on Hayter the only solution was to have one man clearly designated the supreme authority of Vickers & Benson's creative department. That man had to be Philp. Both Terrys agreed.

"As far as I knew he was the only choice," Hayter realized. "It was something that one day just jumped out at me. The key thing for making the vision work was to have somebody committed to making it work, and Philp has great strategic capability. He is by far the most demanding person in here of all the creative people."

And so Philp was appointed executive creative director, and O'Malley and Bell were stripped of all their management duties. They wanted no flashy titles. Copywriter would do nicely. That's all they wanted to be anyway. Leave the meetings and the administration and the headaches to Philp.

In the weeks leading up to the staff announcement, Hayter reworked and polished his presentation. He wanted to make sure that everyone not only understood the rationale for the revamped agency structure, but truly bought into it. Real change would only come if they were as passionate about the new direction as he and the rest of the executive team were.

And so he had to be as thorough in his explanation as possible. He had to give the background reasoning, then gently but firmly lead the staff to reach the same conclusions he had. They had to believe that his course of action was inevitable and correct. Then the agency would be ready to go forward as a united team.

He, of course, would be their coach. And like a coach he prepared all the play-by-play strategies. He had a series of flip charts drawn up that crystallized everything he and the other managers had thrashed out in their meetings.

The presentation would have two components. The first would outline the problems the agency faced. The second, what Vickers & Benson must do to meet the challenges.

After a dry-run with the executive team, Hayter felt rehearsed and ready to face the troops. He called three meetings, to be held one after another in the fifth-floor boardroom. Up first would be the creative department, followed by account management. The third meeting would be for the rest of the staff in administration and services. Each group would get identical presentations.

There was an air of expectation as the creative staff assembled. They knew something big was to be announced. Rumours had been circulating for weeks that a shake-up was imminent, and word had begun to leak that key executives would be making moves. Everyone, naturally, was concerned about what that meant for their own jobs and futures.

The room shushed as Hayter began to speak. Vickers & Benson, he said, had to face up to the fact that advertising as it had been known and practised was undergoing a dramatic revolution, one that would continue to build through the balance of the decade. He pointed to the first chart. Here are the realities:

1. Creativity.

"Increasingly, clients are demanding outstanding creative work. It's very difficult to differentitate your product technologically—to have a Crest with Fluoristat and get an endorsement from a governing body to have an exclusive advantage for a long period of time. The ability to copy any new product or service is almost instantaneous.

"So how you differentiate your product creatively is becoming more important than it has ever been. The soft-drink category used to be just Coca-Cola, Orange Crush and 7Up and a little bit of Pepsi. In the beer business there are dozens of labels you can purchase across Canada. So differentiation, segmentation, requires that you give creative reasons why your product is needed and wanted.

"Creativity is going to be where it's at. And it's going to be especially true for Canadian companies because we don't rework or adapt campaigns done by our corporate headquarters in another country. Everything we do is our work, and if we're not great at it we're not going to succeed. Our attractiveness must be our creative product."

That means client handling is becoming less and less important, he said. In the past, if a client had hotshot MBAs in the marketing department, an agency also had to have hotshot MBAs.

"It's not that way at all now. They're not looking for a mirror image. They're looking for an opposite. We bring these things to the table, you add value to the things we bring to the table. It's driven by the need for ideas to differentiate. And you can't differentiate by copying one another. Your resources have to be additional, not complementary.

"So the implication for us is we have to immediately transform from being a client-handling company to an idea-producing enterprise. That's what we're in business for. This company was a great client handler. We loved our clients. We smothered them."

No more, he said. "Our centre of gravity must be a creative power."

He flipped to the next chart.

2. Revenues.

"Making money under our current structure is going to become more and more difficult. Clients will pay only for value-added services. They don't need us to do the same things they can do."

More ominous, he added, flipping to chart 3., is that there will be low to no growth in client budgets over the next few years.

"We're seeing most budgets decline, certainly in real terms. We can't expect significant increases in budgets for the foreseeable future. So we need more intelligent compensation agreements, especially for value-added work. It used to be when budgets were healthy and you were getting 15 per cent commission you'd throw in sales promotion. We're now a company which is doing much more than just advertising, and 15 per cent compensation can't pay for those services.

"Because budgets aren't growing, clients want new ways to have more impact for their dollar. That puts more stress on us to become innovative and creative and add value. They want more value, but they're not giving us more money for it. That's a major, major reality we have to look at."

4. Accountability.

"Clients now have multiple spending options and they want greater accountablity for where and why they spend their money.

"The problem is that accountability is not a science. You can't say this ad is going to deliver these results. The person who comes up with a formula for that is going to be a very wealthy person. So the potential to create accountability chaos—where each client insists on their method of accountability—could be a major problem."

You could see the worry lines deepening in the room as Hayter moved from one gloom-laden chart to the next. Hayter kept flipping.

5. Integration for some, segregation for others.

"The buzzword is integration," he said. "The reality is some clients are really passionate about buying integration. Others don't give a damn. They want to buy à la carte. In the long run integration will become more important. But you could go broke trying to convince clients that aren't there yet, for whatever reason. If that's what you're serving them, you're not going to be working with them very long.

"So you have to say, all right, we're going to be able to deliver integration where wanted. We're going to be able to deliver à la carte where wanted."

But to service both kinds of clients, Vickers & Benson must be equally strong in each communication skill, Hayter warned. Creatively, there can be no weak links.

Flip to the next chart.

6. We can't afford integration as presently practised.

"I don't think there's an agency in Canada that can," Hayter said. "There aren't the dollars there. Revenues from our integrated resources are insufficient to profitably afford totally independent infrastructures. You can't have a full acount-service department for advertising, a full account-service department that would handle promotion. Or direct marketing. The critical mass or the size of the budgets just aren't there. They're there in the United States for some clients, but not all. But they're certainly not here."

The implication? Vickers & Benson must develop a new kind of account person, a generalist who understands advertising, direct marketing, sales promotion and public relations. Someone who will then be able to advise clients on all those areas.

"What we want is a new breed," Hayter said. "The agency that gets there first—and really does it—is going to have a competitive edge."

At the same time, he added, Vickers & Benson must make better use of the large talent pool of creative freelancers, especially those experts in specialized disciplines who can be called in to work on short-term projects as needed.

"That will allow us to do integration more affordably than we have in the past. We've tried to do it by having everything in-house, and the math doesn't add up."

Flip to 7. Globalization.

"I think that trend is there, and it's not going to go away," Hayter continued. "It'll probably slow down, but it's still a trend. We know that the mission of global companies is to create global products with global efficiencies. For many, this will translate to continual consolidation of marketing and advertising services with global agencies.

"So the implication is, short term, some client opportunities for us may go away. The chances to compete for new business may shrink for us."

Flip.

8. Freer trade could open up government business to global agencies.

It was extremely improbable that the new Liberal government would alter the policy of only awarding ad contracts to agencies that are majority Canadian controlled, Hayter said. Nonetheless, Vickers & Benson would be foolish to count on government business as a revenue mainstay.

"It is opportunistic, it allows you to expand, it allows you to create a talent base. But it will come and go. There's always a beginning and an end to that."

Vickers & Benson, he reminded them, had long ties with a number of its clients. More than thirty years with Ford, twenty-five with 3M, twenty-seven with the Ontario Jockey Club, fourteen with McDonald's.

"That will never happen with a government piece of business, so you should never rely on it."

Finally, Hayter flipped to the last chart in this portion of his presentation. The staff listened attentively as he identified the most critical point of all.

"We must have a unified vision, one that we believe in and unites us and inspires us and drives us. A unified belief in how to attack the future can multiply our results. And if we are not united, we will divide. Multiplication beats division every time."

He turned from his charts.

"We have camps," he said, his eyes moving from face to face around the room. "We have old V&Bers. We have new V&Bers. We have it in the creative department and we have it in account management. We have it everywhere! That will not play.

"What plays is our vision of what we're going to be. Everything we do must be to drive that. We're all contributors to that. Some are greater contributors; some are lesser contributors. But we're all contributors."

He paused to let the words sink in. There were nods and murmurs of approval, and a few flushed faces. Satisfied that everyone understood why it was so important why they—why the whole agency—must adapt to the changing market-place, Hayter moved on to the second half of his presentation.

It is imperative, he began, that Vickers & Benson reposition and restructure itself into a company that is committed to delivering break-through creative work.

"That may sound obvious," he said, "but there are not many companies that really are in that business. Most of us are compromised. We've been compromised. We've been good client handlers. We believe in doing great work, and try hard to do it. But we don't get up in the morning and say, 'Dammit, I'm here to develop ideas and drive our clients' business. That's all I want. That's all I care about.'"

And if that means telling a client to stop handing out meaningless duties that rob time from the real work of solving problems, have the guts to do it, Hayter said.

"If you have that as your vision you will be more likely to eliminate those things that prevent you from developing ideas that can drive the business."

He hammered home the point.

"Administrivia will prevent us from being what we want to be. Being an idea-producing enterprise that creates results will make us great and our clients more successful."

He flipped to another chart, this one showing a drawing of a nebula swirling around two words: CREATIVE POWERHOUSE.

Everybody wants V&B to be known for its creative prowess, he conceded. But Vickers & Benson must aim higher. It should be the agency that everybody on the street envies. Each new campaign breaks through the clutter, and sets a new high standard for the category.

"That's what a powerhouse is," Hayter said. "When they're talking about the work you do for your clients. Not just the work you do. But the work you do for your clients. Because we are in the business of making our clients succeed."

Hayter shrugged. Will people actually use the words "creative powerhouse" to describe Vickers & Benson? Of course they won't.

"But they will talk about us in the context that we have great work that drives our client. They will not talk about clients generally. They'll talk about specifics. They'll say, 'Did you see that campaign for Gatorade or Molson? Isn't that great?'

"That's what we want."

So if the vision is to become a creative powerhouse, the strategy must then be to develop the power sources to get there, Hayter said. It means the agency's capabilities in all disciplines must be upgraded. It is no longer enough just to provide excellence in advertising. The same level of expertise has to be there in direct marketing, public relations and corporate design.

"There's a need to come around and whack the other guy from the other side. And if we don't have the power sources to pull it off all we can do is retreat to a one-dimensional, or two- or three-dimensional, solution. Once we do that, we are asking the client to compromise.

"Or we're trying to sell the client something that is not the right solution. Or the client's going to go and look for someone else because we're not providing that solution. We're not getting outside the box. We're not getting outside our comfort zone."

And so it went for the rest of Hayter's presentation. As he flipped his charts, his tone would darken as he admonished his staff to face up to the new realities of an industry in flux. Then he would temper his admonitions with predictions of glory—if the necessary changes were made.

Revenue and service plans must be developed for each client. The account management department has to be flattened to two levels. One for idea-producers, the other for administrators and co-ordinators.

The talk then turned to salaries and bonuses, a subject that commanded sharp attention. There will be a new compensation system, Hayter announced. "Right now we do not have an incentive program. We're working on that. We will be compensating according to performance. It could be a combination of great work and the financial success of an account. There will be no automatic salary increases."

With that topic out of the way, Hayter was ready to discuss even bigger changes. There would be new units set up to target emerging communication needs. Joe Warwick would be in charge of sports and entertainment marketing. A deal was pending with a Toronto firm, Vandenberg & Associates, to provide expertise in corporate identity and packaging design.

And another thing, Hayter told the group. There must be a concerted effort to implement a plan to acquire only accounts that meet with the new mandate.

"Right now we try to be disciplined, but too often we'll go after an account and then think about whether we should have or not," he said. "Compatibility in any relationship is key, and we often don't even think about it. Will they allow us to be what we want to be? If we are different things to different clients because we want to have the business then we have no vision. The vision is to be whatever you have to be. Be a chameleon. And that is not our vision."

And while we're on the topic, why not form liaisons with privately owned agencies in other countries that share our vision? he asked.

"Our ultimate goal is to be a creative powerhouse globally. Why not work with a top creative agency in the U.K.? They have a need just like we do. They're equally vulnerable to the global agencies."

But first things first. Vickers & Benson must get its own house in order before it could entertain the notion of building an international network. And that has to start with the creative department, the core of the agency's operation, he said.

Effective immediately, Hayter announced, Philp is executive creative director. O'Malley and Bell will devote their energies and talents to writing ads.

There was a collective gasp. Some in the room had suspected Philp was earmarked for the top. One or two had even been told in confidence to expect it. But hearing it publicly made all the difference. There would be no turning back.

The creatives applauded their new boss, then, a little shell-shocked, rose from their seats and exited the boardroom. Hayter flipped his charts back to the beginning and waited for the next group to file in.

# CHAPTER 9

I T WAS ONE THING to claim the agency was striving to become a creative powerhouse; quite another to see how Philp and the rest of the creative department would make it happen.

As chance would have it, they got an early opportunity to prove their mettle with the launch of Molson Breweries' Signature Series of premium beers. Ironically, Philp almost didn't have a role in the ad campaign, which was launched only weeks after the announcement of his appointment.

It all started in early 1993, when Don Lum, Molson's director of product development, made a surprise call on Hayter. The brewery was looking for an agency with the creative smarts to handle a hush-hush project, one so big that it would be pivotal to Molson's marketing future.

The fact that Bell and Gordon were working together once again was one of the draws that brought him to Vickers & Benson. Lum had known Bell for years. Before joining Molson, he was with Ralston

Purina, the pet food company, whose agency was Scali McCabe Sloves, Bell's employer in the 1980s. Lum knew Gordon when the art director was at MacLaren Advertising, one of Molson's agencies.

Lum was impressed with the work Vickers & Benson had done on the Amstel account, he told Hayter. And he was anxious to work with Bell and Gordon on this new project, the launch of two beers under the new Signature Series label. But he stressed he did not want to be buried under layers of account managers. He could always get that kind of client handling from his other agencies. Keep things neat and stream-lined and he would gladly give Vickers & Benson the assignment.

Hayter was ecstatic. If they did a good job on this project, it might lead to bigger assignments from Molson. That was one of his goals, to become known as one of the brewer's mainstream agencies. The pres-tige that would bring, let alone the added revenue, would certainly make the market-place sit up and take notice that Vickers & Benson was once again a force to be reckoned with.

He had one request of Lum, however. He wanted him to allow Philp, who was then still the director of client services, to help on the project.

Philp was not the typical client handler, Hayter insisted. He was really a brilliant strategist with a strong creative bent. He would be the perfect complement to Bell and Gordon. Vickers & Benson would even pick up the tab for his services if Molson would permit him to be part of the team.

Lum initially balked at the idea, but was finally convinced that Philp could be an asset if he functioned more like a creative planner—some-one who provided strategic insight and guidance—rather than an account manager.

Everyone involved knew how important this campaign would be to the agency's future. The company had proven its stuff on the Amstel and Heineken brands, both distributed in Canada by Molson. But this would mark the first time that Vickers & Benson would get to work on products bearing Molson's name.

There was a sense that the creative team had to go beyond the call of duty and come up with a campaign that would knock Molson flat. The pressure of bopping a home run over the fence was palpable, Philp said. "You felt that responsibility every day."

Lum told the team that Molson decided to launch the Signature Series label based on research indicating a trend to drinkers buying "change of pace" beers for special occasions. There was a time that wasn't the case. People had a favourite brew and they stuck to it. But increasingly, a sizeable segment of drinkers—most of them educated, boomer-aged men—were reaching for a microbrewery-produced premium beer to slake their thirsts. If they liked what they tasted, they would add it to their menu of beer choices.

The development clearly concerned Molson. If the brewer didn't then have a beer to keep loyal customers in the fold, it would invent one. It would be made in small batches from the finest malts without any preservatives. Walter Hogg, Molson's brewmaster, was commissioned to find the right recipe. He came up with an ale and a lager that were good enough that he would sign his name to the labels.

Meanwhile, Molson was brewing a plan to launch the beers in flamboyant style. They would be introduced not as just two additions to the brand roster. Rather, they would be the linchpins of a new marketing thrust, to be unveiled at a news conference with the now-requisite blare of rock music and splashy video.

On October 28, Bruce Pope, Molson's president and chief executive officer, took to the stage of a dance theatre on Toronto's waterfront to proclaim the arrival of the new label. But he didn't stop there.

He also announced that henceforth all Molson products would be made without preservatives. All packaging would list a toll-free 1-800 hotline number consumers could call with complaints or compliments. Finally, Molson would help bars and licensed restaurants get discounts on insurance, computers and other products and services.

It was all part of Molson's commitment to better service, based on a year-long customer probe, Pope said.

"This was the largest research program undertaken in Molson's history," he told reporters. "We listened to what more than fifteen thousand consumers, as well as thousands of bar and restaurant owners, had to say."

As part of the hoopla attending the launch of all these initiatives, Vickers & Benson was readying two separate campaigns. The first was a newspaper ad. It featured two illustrations. At the top of the page was a picture of a mountain poking through clouds. At the bottom of the page was a Molson bottle cap.

IN YOUR DREAMS read the underlined headline. Beneath that, some of Bell's more grandiose philosophic musings:

"In your dreams you ask how high is up? How good am I? How good can I be? Can I be great? In our dreams we ask the very same questions. And we're about to find out."

The copy went on to talk about the new preservative-free policy, the launch of the Signature label, a new product guarantee and the 1-800 number.

The ad ended with a flourish:

"In our dreams we have this vision of being your brewer. This too will be a reality." Finally, a new tag-line: "Molson. Dare To Be Great."

The Vickers & Benson team were saving their heaviest bombast for the actual brand launch. It would be unlike any other beer advertising the agency, or indeed any agency, had produced.

The creative team knew that the new label needed more than the usual party-time pap served up as beer advertising. Research was showing that consumers, sparked by the politically correct advance guard of feminist groups like Media Watch and government bureaucrats, were tiring of the tits-and-ass approach brewers had long embraced.

Indeed, savvy beermakers were already catching on to the sea change in public opinion. The most striking example was a TV commercial created by the Geoffrey Roche ad agency for Sleeman Brewing & Malting Co. Ltd., a Guelph, Ontario-based microbrewer. It ran in the spring and summer prior to the Signature launch.

The Sleeman ad had great fun turning the beer-ad cliché on its head.

"Our market research department," the announcer intoned, "said the best way to sell beer was to do a commercial showing lots of women in sexy bikinis hanging all over the guys. So we asked our staff at the brewery what they thought. The men were into it. But the women refused to wear bikinis and hang all over the men they work with."

Pregnant pause to set up the gag. "We no longer have a market research department."

The Vickers & Benson team was also sensitive to the beer-and-bimbo tag. No way was Signature to be loaded with that sort of sexist baggage. But there was more to it than that.

Research also showed that consumers were wearying of the beer wars, the never-ending feud between Molson and arch-rival Labatt Breweries. Consumers were also beginning to feel that the big industry players were no longer practising the time-honoured craft of brewing beer. They were merely manufacturing the stuff like any other disposable consumer good.

Brands were being launched with bewildering speed and regularity.

Molson came out with a dry beer only to be matched by Labatt, which came out with a draft beer only to be seconded by Molson. Ice beers led to extra-strength beers led to low-cost beers. It was all marketing. Where was the art?

Vickers & Benson's campaign would try to set the record straight that a big brewer like Molson still had the wherewithal to brew the best.

But how to do that persuasively? Molson is the country's biggest brewer, with huge plants, more than 4,500 employees and a roster of more than forty brands of beer. Would consumers believe this monolith capable of producing top-quality, small-batch beer that rivalled anything the cottage industry of microbrewers churned out?

The Vickers & Benson team felt the only way to accomplish the task was to play it straight. There would be no attempt to hide the fact that mighty Molson was behind the new beers. The answer, it was decided, was to highlight the fact that the brewery had the heritage and skills necessary to make beers of this quality.

But to do that effectively, they needed a credible spokesman, a symbol of Molson's beer-making craft. Who better than Walter Hogg, the brewmaster?

The more they thought about it, the more convinced the creative team was that Hogg was the right man. They struck on an innovative concept to play up his credibility. If Hogg was a true craftsman of the brewing art, why not surround him with craftsmen from other professions? By association, Hogg would then be seen in an even more flattering light.

Bell and Gordon brainstormed likely candidates. They came up with a number of possibilities, finally winnowing the list to four. Each would be highlighted in the ad campaign, due to begin in late November.

The men they chose are all masters of their craft. George Aslanidis is a

Greek cobbler; Corrado Accaputo, an Italian barber; Wayne Martin, a custom fly-rod maker; and Grit Laskin, a legendary guitar maker.

Philp thought them ideal choices. "It was the judgment of the creative team that that particular combination of crafts felt right, and Canadian enough and natural enough and accessible enough," he said.

Picking Accaputo was inspired, he added. He is just a simple barber, proud of his skill. Someone any beer drinker could relate to.

The craftsmen's stories are told in a sumptuous eight-page newspaper insert that kicked off the campaign.

The first page of insert shows a tall, sweating glass of beer, the head foaming down one side. "How do you know when you've brewed a great beer?" the copy asks. Turn the page and find a picture of Aslanidis working on a cowboy boot. "Ask a Bootmaker," the headline reads.

"You could bring your world weary shoes to George Aslanidis, the ones with that big yawn in the right sole," the copy begins. "The ones that you lived in all summer and now lay exhausted and spent at the bottom of your closet."

The copy goes on to talk at length about the bootmaker's craft, philosophy and dedication. There is nary a word about beer.

"Ask a Barber," the headline on the following page reads. Again, long copy about skill and pride. And no mention of beer. Instead, there's a sensuous description of the perfect shave:

"The kind of shaves you used to see in all those old western and gangster movies. The kind of shave that takes time and patience and leaves your face with the texture of a cue ball. To accomplish this, Corrado will first apply to your face a moisturizing cream. Next, he will liberally apply a hot shave foam. By now you're starting to feel as mellow as a man can in an upright position. Get used to it."

And so on for two more pages, each with profiles of the rod maker and guitar man. But nothing about beer.

Then, on page six, we see a smiling face of Hogg. "Ask a Brewmaster," the headline reads. "Walter Hogg has never made a pair of boots or crafted his own 12-string guitar or given anybody a close shave," the copy begins. "But as Molson's premier brewmaster, he can relate totally to Grit Laskin, George Aslanidis and Corrado Accaputo. What he relates to most is their desire for excellence, their passion for their craft, their daring to be great."

With that connection made, the copy then describes the new brews. The copy ends with the signature line of the Signature Series: "Passion. The daring to be great. If you can spot it in life you'll spot it in our new line of Signature Series beers. You have our brewmaster's word on it."

Using a soft-sell newspaper insert like this is rare in the hyped-up world of beer marketing. But Lum was sure that, for this new line at least, the approach was right.

"We wanted to communicate with our customers in a manner that was both direct and intimate to set the stage for the entire campaign," he said. "That required a long-copy format. The insert allowed us to create a piece that was beautifully crafted—to look at and to read—which is another way of communicating the passion and dedication it takes to be a true craftsperson."

That same attitude permeates the four thirty-second TV commercials that began airing shortly after the insert came out. Once again, there's Accaputo rhapsodizing about the perfect shave, Laskin quietly philosophizing about making guitars and Martin fly-fishing in a sun-dappled stream. Hogg talks about passion and craftsmanship and the need for both to make quality beer.

He is also featured in a cheeky newspaper ad with the eye-catching headline, "Sorry, Walter." The brewmaster is pictured half out of the frame, as if he truly were embarrassed to be in the ad.

"If Walter had his way, you'd never be reading this ad," the copy states. "He is not big on advertising. Never has been. The way Walter sees it, the smartest thing we could do would be to simply ask all our good friends to get hold of a six pack and let them decide for themselves."

Nice thought, the non-advertising ad continues. "Unfortunately for Walter, Molson has a marketing department."

The copy then extols the virtues of the new Signature Series' Cream Ale and Amber Lager in typical Adland fashion. The tongue-in-cheek tone picks up again half-way down the page.

"For this, our marketing department told Walter you need advertising. For this, Walter said you need a couple of chilled glasses and a couple of good friends."

As might be expected, the beer launch attracted the scornful attention of the microbrewers, who accused Molson of muscling in on their turf. Frank Heaps, president of Upper Canada Brewing Co., was particularly incensed.

"They seem to be trying to convince the public that they're as natural as an Upper Canada or another micro, when in fact they're not," he complained to *The Financial Post*. "The drinking public should be very careful and scrutinize what is being marketed here. It is not microbrewery quality beer."

It fell to Freda Colbourne from Molson's public-relations department to counter the negative press.

There was certainly no intention to mislead the public, she assured. The Signature Series beers were specifically designed for Molson drinkers who, on occasion, might stray when they wanted to try something a little different.

"We're hoping that they're going to stay within the 'family' because we're going to be able to offer them that different sort of premium-type positioning and taste with the Cream Ale and Amber Lager. We do have the brewing credentials within our family to do that, to be able to brew this type of beer.

"Somebody who is an Upper Canada drinker probably wouldn't want to come over and try our beers anyway."

Despite the flap, which was short-lived, Philp was delighted not only with the finished product, but the process of creating the campaign.

"Two things make this campaign really exciting for us," he said. "First, this is advertising that celebrates real people and some downright noble values. That's rare in any product category, and it really gave the advertising its heart. It also makes it very rewarding to work on.

"Second, the process was a terrific example of the new thinking at Vickers & Benson. We had a very small team of senior people involved in the project right from the product concept stage. There were no boundaries, no bureaucracy, no handling. We were very accountable for our contribution, yet we always felt like we were part of Molson's team. I think that shows in the work."

Molson was equally pleased with the campaign, and the initial reception in the market-place.

"We did some quantitative research," Lum said. "We moved the dial on all the scores that we were looking for, so we have a high degree of confidence."

The bonus was that Molson's own employees were rallying around the new beers. "It's very interesting to see how it's taking hold internally," he said. "It's something you'd be proud to serve your friends and your relatives."

After the campaign hit the streets, Lum called Philp to thank the

Vickers & Benson team for work well done. "I trust you like no other agency I've worked with," he said.

Later, after Philp was made executive creative director, Hayter dashed a note off to Lum. "I told you he was a creative guy," he wrote.

# CHAPTER 10

O'MALLEY'S AGREEMENT to step down as executive creative director in favour of Philp was a turning point for Vickers & Benson. It meant that the rifts in the staff ranks could slowly begin to heal.

Finally, after two years of tension between the old guard and the new breed, it was clear in which direction the agency was headed, and who was at the helm. Hayter, along with his hand-picked team of managers, was now firmly in control.

But it was a bruising triumph, and victory was never certain.

As long as O'Malley, who was never really sure he wanted to sell the agency in the first place, remained sphinx-like in his fifth-floor office—a "hall of fame" with trophies, sports memorabilia and the sundry mementoes chronicling a milestone thirty-year career—he was a threat to Hayter's authority.

It wasn't as if he was being deliberately obstructive. On the contrary, O'Malley had bent over backwards not to impede Hayter's day-to-day operation of the firm. But his mere presence proved to be a disrupting influence, rallying the loyalists and frustrating those who were striving for change.

He had become a ghostly figure, always hovering in the background, never opposing, never disturbing. But still tremendously influential.

"The fifth floor is haunted by Terry O'Malley," David Hurst, the consultant hired to break the impasse, reported after his initial assessment.

"Although he is actively trying not to interfere, trying not to get in the way of John, the fact is most of what managers do is through body language anyway. And by doing nothing, that sends a message."

"Terry," he added, "does not like to confront people or issues. It's not a role he has had to play. Bill Bremner, his partner, did that for him, and allowed Terry to do what he's good at, which is creating. When Bill's priorities changed and he left the scene, the organization was left rudderless."

Hayter came in as captain, but he had been hampered by economic circumstances beyond his control. O'Malley was to receive money for his shares based on the agency's financial performance. The company was essentially buying him out. But the recession had cut deep into profits, delaying his promised pay-out.

If O'Malley had insisted on an upfront cash deal, no doubt he would have long since left the firm. Hayter, meantime, would have had a much freer hand in rebuilding the agency.

"But instead it's like a dance conducted with everybody standing in a foot of treacle," Hurst observed. "It's very slow. Things that should have been easy are actually difficult and embarrassing."

The result? A reluctance to confront tough issues because neither party felt secure in their positions. O'Malley didn't want to upset the deal, but he was concerned about the pace of the transaction. Hayter was a natural bridge between the new breed and the old camp. But that meant O'Malley would have to step aside. Until he did, substantive change would be impossible.

"They're paralyzed," Hurst concluded. "It is a logjam—and Terry O'Malley is the absolute key to unlocking that jam."

"What sort of guy is O'Malley? Well, if I had to write an epitaph for him I'd choose: 'Here lies a great humanitarian and intellectual who died with his jockstrap on.'"

That's how Bremner once described his long-time partner.

Others share the same view. O'Malley is widely admired as a brilliant copywriter, a consummate athlete, an impeccable dresser. But he is also seen as an intensely private, enigmatic individual.

Elizabeth Watson, who profiled O'Malley after he had been named president of Vickers & Benson, described her first meeting in a 1975 *Marketing* article:

"Sitting in his large, cluttered office on V&B's creative floor (where he intends to remain), O'Malley looks the way you'd expect him to.

"He's wearing a blue-and-orange, plaid seersucker jacket. And two-tone shoes. Despite stern brushing, his hair is unruly. His eyes are water-green under bushy brows, and he's got this fine, virile mustache bristling under a strong nose.

"He's lean and hard-bellied as all good jocks should be.

"Considering the larger-than-life reputation he has in the industry and the Irish-rogue look of the man, it comes as a bit of shock to discover that O'Malley in conversation merely projects (and wants to project) nothing more than a pleasant, low-key image.

"Nobody had told me that the guy is shy!"

Almost two decades later, O'Malley still sends out those same contradictory messages, of strength intermingled with tentativeness.

It would be easy to confuse his soft-spoken manner with ingenuousness. In fact, he is that rarest of hybrids, a philosopher who is also a man of action. A poet and fitness fanatic. A deep thinker with the competitive instinct of a marathon runner.

"I'm not the kind of guy who's content doing things half-way," he said in a 1989 interview with *The Financial Post*. "It's all or nothing. For races, I'd push really hard in training, and that would leave me wide open to injury."

To O'Malley, the ad game is just that, a game. He looks at the business through the eyes of a disciplined athlete who is not afraid to go the distance. Someone with the dedication to jog at least six miles for a thousand straight days, a goal he achieved in the summer of 1982.

When O'Malley analyzes his profession, he leans heavily on the language of sports.

"You have to be sensitive without being too sensitive," he once told *The Toronto Star*. "I call that being professional, being able to have perspective on things. After all, you're not discovering America when you come up with a great line.

"The hard part is realizing that the industry is like sports. One year you're big and you command a huge salary. Next year, you can be out with nothing. You're only as good as your last piece of work.

"There are no guarantees. You don't work for 20 years and feel assured of a steady salary just because you hung in."

O'Malley, who was born and raised in St. Catharines, Ontario, had a precarious childhood.

"My father was into everything from owning a soap company to selling urinal screens," he recalled in the 1975 *Marketing* profile. "One day I was being chauffeured to private school, the next I was in the back of a panel truck escaping angry creditors."

He graduated from high school at sixteen, and went off to Harvard University on an academic scholarship. Following that, he enrolled in a Master of Arts program in English at the University of Toronto.

At age twenty-two, he joined MacLaren Advertising, earning fifty dollars a week to write ad copy for General Motors. He reminisced about his first brush with the ad business in a 1985 article he wrote for *The Financial Post*:

"It was just about the end of my first year working on a master's degree at University of Toronto. I borrowed a grey '56 Chevy from a friend of my mother's in St. Catharines, and talked one of my closest friends into coming to Toronto with my girlfriend and me while she applied for a job at Kodak. We parked on Richmond St. and while she had her interview, my friend urged me to start looking for a summer job.

"I went into a building, read the registry and it was a toss-up between Zurich Insurance and MacLaren Advertising. Another of my St. Catharines pack had worked at MacLaren, so I gave it a try.

"[Receptionist] Shirley Mitchell greeted me and asked what I'd like to do. A little bewildered (I thought companies did their own ads; I didn't know what an agency did), I asked 'What is there?' She suggested account work, media, research, art direction, copywriting, production and so on. Copywriting sounded good. At least it was relative to the English I was studying."

So began one of the most illustrious careers in Canadian advertising.

O'Malley wrote about those early years in an article for *Marketing*. It was at MacLaren, he wrote, that he met his mentors. The first was Doug Murray, the agency's creative head.

"A brusque, aggressive, handsome man with a crushing handshake. Fortunately, he liked poetry. In the next year, Doug pushed me to explore every idea I could conceive. He'd tell me the how but it was always up to me to know the why. There weren't any writer-art director teams, so you worked independently. Doug encouraged me to do my own layouts. He let me talk and deal directly with the studio.

"The work was pouring out. I was a prolific fat kid in a corduroy suit. Doug also had this sense of eccentricity which always intrigued me. You'd be reading a script to him while he was feeding flies to his Venus Flytrap plant. Get the picture?"

Ted Wood, MacLaren's copy chief, was O'Malley's second mentor.

"Before I was hired, Ted called me or whoever would get the junior's job Shithead because he felt the money ($50 a week) should have gone in raises," O'Malley wrote. "Ted was a tough Englishman and an ex-Metro beat cop who had written ads and stuff on the backs of tickets to get hired at the agency.

"He made me appreciate the pleasure of words. Words to him were friends, playthings, amazing bits of energy and wit that one could combine in all kinds of ways to bring joy, meaning and creativity. He was stern. He was difficult (every time I'd bring in a piece of copy, before he even began reading, he'd take out a sharpened red pencil and poise it over the page).

"He was a perfectionist. He didn't want to be like anyone else, and he wanted me to be that way, too. Don't copy, originate, was always his message to me. It was an intense group. We did all kinds of ads in print and broadcast and sales promotion. I was there a year and a half. The effect I still feel today."

After that colourful start at MacLaren, O'Malley went on to do stints at Young & Rubicam and Foster Advertising, where he met Bremner.

The two left to join Vickers & Benson in 1964. Bremner was put in charge of special promotions. O'Malley, who was then twenty-eight, was hired as a creative group head.

By 1975, he was president, a significant achievement for someone who came from the creative ranks since, typically, the presidential suite is reserved for those with an account-management background.

Then came the 1980s, and what O'Malley describes today as the "feeding frenzy" of mergers and buy-outs that transformed the agency business worldwide. As one of the last remaining holdouts, Vickers & Benson was a frequent target of numerous unsolicited deals.

Many of the proposals came from "loonies" with improbable schemes. At the height of the frenzy, letters inundated his office. "They'd be under my door when I came in in the morning," he recalls.

Once when the agency was being courted by NW Ayer, an American firm, he, Bremner and several other V&B executives were invited to visit their New York headquarters.

O'Malley has vivid memories of what turned out to be a surrealistic comedy of errors.

"I said to Bill, 'What's the difference between renting an airplane and flying regular coach?' It was like three hundred bucks, so we took this jet down to Newark, where we were picked up by limo and we went down to Ayer's offices.

"They said, 'Before we start we want to make sure we cover everything. What time is your return flight?' Bill said, 'It's okay. We have the jet.'

"It was just unbelievable! It was like all of a sudden we went from being these hicks to 'Oh, really...?'"

The meeting over, the Vickers & Benson team took the limousine back to the airport.

"We had done this through a charter company, and expected we'd be billed [for the car]. So we all get out of the car and start walking towards the aircraft. All of a sudden, the limo driver starts yelling for security because we didn't pay him.

"We're saying, 'We're sorry, we didn't know.' There's six of us, but with varying amounts of American money, trying to collect enough to pay this guy.

"Bill's got it, and he's dropping money in the wind and it's blowing away. There were guys in suits chasing dollar bills across the tarmac!"

O'Malley laughs uproariously at the absurdity of the situation, at the symbolism of bills wafting just out of reach.

Then came the 1990s and the recession and Hayter knocking on his door. He was looking to return to Canada after his corporate adventures abroad in Britain and the United States.

Hayter wanted a piece of the action, and O'Malley and Bremner, after long months of negotiation, finally agreed. Hayter would buy into the firm, and become president and CEO. O'Malley would sit back to collect his due for the years of dedication and toil. He is still waiting.

"God knows if I'll ever get my money out of here," he says ruefully.

"If it collapsed, I would lose all the investment I have put in over thirty years."

Before he turned the creative department over to Philp, O'Malley says he was in limbo. It felt as though he was the only guy in the room without a script.

For a moment, the weight of the memory seems crushing. Then, just as quickly, he brightens, and the philosopher-jock is back in stride.

"My theory of advertising is the best you can get is a tie. No one will ever give you credit for a win. It can't be the advertising, it has to be marketing, or the distribution, or the sales force, or whatever.

"If it doesn't work, it's the advertising. So that wears you down after awhile.

"I like to have guys who play sports be in this business with me. Because the key thing about being an athlete is you learn from losing.

Losing isn't disastrous. It's just another step in the process. Many times, you win as you lose.

"You can lose a hockey game ten to one, but during the course of that you might have won five face-offs. You might have beaten the guy to the puck that you've never got to before. You still didn't win, but next time you're going to improve.

"That's the terrific part about this. Sometimes at your lowest ebb you score. There's nothing more exhilarating."

In his teen years, Hayter was also a star athlete. He still likes to play hard, and to win.

As a kid growing up in Toronto, he was big for his age, excelling at football, baseball, hockey. He became a champion runner. He was also dyslexic, compensating for his insecurities and low grades by becoming the class clown.

"I was a goof-off," he says. "I was the smart aleck, the guy with all the flip answers. I was a jock. I didn't give a shit."

His father's premature death put an abrupt halt to the tomfoolery. At the age of seventeen, he became the man of the house. After spending a year at the University of New Brunswick, where he played running back, he returned to Toronto in 1961 to join Spitzer Mills & Bates as a research assistant. He started at the bottom making fifty-eight dollars a week.

He thrust himself into his new-found career, eventually becoming an executive on the Colgate account, working upwards of a hundred hours a week. Facing early burn-out, he quit to join J. Walter Thompson, where he was assigned the Alberto-Culver account. At the age of twenty-seven, he crossed over to the client side to become the soap company's sales and marketing manager for Canada. By the time he was thirty, he was managing director of the ailing London office.

It was an eye-opening experience for him. He remembers going into the office the first day and meeting his very British salesmen, all much older than him, dressed in starched shirts and bowler hats. Sales were down, competition was intense, and here were his staff sauntering in late, sitting down at their desks to read the morning paper! Hayter was aghast. He fired the deadwood and began taking charge.

New products were introduced, better distribution channels were opened up. Hayter even remembers loading up his car to deliver stock to stores himself. But the hard work paid off. By the time he left England, Alberto-Culver was number two in shampoo sales, and number one in conditioner sales.

Hayter thinks back fondly. It was tough sledding at work, but the social life was incomparable. It was a whirlwind of fancy clubs and luxury cars. With his tax breaks and U.S. salary he could afford to buy a beautiful sixteenth-century home.

He remembers how proud he was when he bought a Jaguar. He shakes his head at the memory. "Who here in Canada in 1971 at the age of thirty had a Jag?" he marvels.

Head office was impressed by the turnaround Hayter wrought. In 1980 he was rewarded with a big promotion as the chief of the grocery household products division in the U.S. It was not what Hayter expected or wanted. Being so close to headquarters cramped his style, and he felt smothered by the tight control of the family-run operation. He quit the firm, crossed the street and took over the presidency of Young & Rubicam's Chicago office.

Here, too, Hayter made his mark. Y&R prospered under his leadership. The agency had a string of new-business wins, and cultivated a strong roster of accounts—Miller Brewing Co., International Harvester and Navistar among them. During his tenure, the agency's billings tripled from $40 million to $120 million.

Feeling that he had taken Y&R as far as he could, and itching for yet another challenge—this time as his own boss—he left Young & Rubicam in 1987 to set up a firm to seek out investment opportunities. By 1989, he was in Canada checking out the Toronto ad scene.

Gary Alles, a school chum who worked at Vickers & Benson in the 1970s, arranged for him to meet Bremner and O'Malley. Bremner said the agency was looking for a president. Would Hayter be interested? Not unless he could get a piece of the action and the authority to make substantive changes, Hayter responded. It took almost two years to hammer out a deal.

After he became president, he realized just how far Vickers & Benson had to go to remain competitive in a business traumatized by recession and cutbacks.

"We're not hungry enough," he says, the old football spirit still burning. We've got to become far more passionate, take our gloves off and get a little animal instinct in us."

The tough talk doesn't entirely convince. There is a vulnerable side that sometimes emerges when he becomes introspective. "I try to be too much of a gentleman," he says, shouldering the blame for his self-perceived faults. "I am intense. I am a competitor. But maybe I have to become a little bit more off-the-wall. Because the Vickers & Benson way has been to be gentlemanly. Always the high road. I want the high road. I just don't want anybody to pass us on the high road."

Terry Bell is on his hobby-horse, railing against one of his pet peeves—the endless round of meetings that keep him from doing the thing he is paid to do, which is to write ads.

"I think we as an industry are often our own worst enemies," he fumes. "Could you imagine if you took the people who designed auto-mobiles or who made automobiles on the assembly line and they spent all that time in meetings instead of turning out a car? Well, we turn out the equivalent of cars. We turn out ads. That's where the time should be spent. That's where the focus should be."

If Bell sounds like a man in a hurry, that's because there has always been a bit of a rebel streak running through him.

Bell got into the ad business by accident. A poor student—he failed grades nine and ten—he dropped out of his Etobicoke high school in grade eleven. He had no idea what he wanted to do, but he was impatient to get on with whatever life held for him.

"We had next-door neighbours whose son was an account supervisor at Vickers & Benson. And he said me, 'Well, you like to write, maybe you can write advertising.'"

He made an appointment to see Bremner. "I was waxing philosophically about life and quoting from Plato and Cicero," he recalls, a blush colouring his cheeks. "He must have thought who is this kid? He called me back and said there's nothing here. But you could start in the mail-room. So I said okay."

So the fresh-faced eighteen-year-old started pushing a mailcart, making forty-five dollars a week. Eventually, Bremner promoted him to junior account executive on the CCM sports account. That was fun for awhile, but what he really wanted to do was switch to the creative side. When he was approached by a small firm looking for a writer, he leapt at the chance.

It was a good apprenticeship, but the job was leading nowhere. And that was a destination he was anxious to avoid. So he jumped ship to McConnell Advertising. Then he got an offer from Vickers & Benson, this time to be a writer. He happily came home. By 1978, he was associate creative director.

But other offers tempted, and never one to resist, he took off again. First to MacLaren, then Foster, then back to MacLaren. By 1985, he was at Scali McCabe Sloves, attracted by the agency's iconoclastic chairman, Gary Prouk, whom Bell hero-worshipped. Still does in a way, even though the relationship has soured. A tragedy for Bell, since Prouk is one of his two mentors. O'Malley is the other. "Terry taught me about grace," Bell says, "and Gary taught me about fire."

Indeed, at first Scali seemed more like Hell.

"My first eight months were absolutely brutal. I had heard stories about how Gary could be particularly hard on writers, more than art directors. It became infinitely better for me the day I pushed back, the day I said, 'Fuck this, I don't need this shit.' It was like a door opened."

He would spend five years at Scali, producing some of the agency's best work on the high-profile Labatt's Blue business. When that account went up for review, Bell and his art director partner, John Speakman, worked feverishly to prepare a winning strategy.

The day of the presentation, they were so keyed up they each popped a Valium. Then they took another.

"We had it choreographed. What I was going to do was the whole pre-amble, the whole rationale, and take them through what we were doing and introduce the theme, 'Play For Real.' I'm doing this and I'm looking around the room and I'm figuring I'm on a roll. We've got something happening here. People are lighting up."

Then it was Speakman's turn. "He stood up and said, 'Good morning, gentlemen. Now I'm going to take you through this stuff...' And people are going, 'Can you speak up a bit, John?' Well, that Valium had kicked in. So John says sure and he starts all over again. And he says [shouting], 'Today I'm going to talk about this...' And his voice just starts to trail off again. People are leaning forward and cupping their ears."

Despite their Laurel & Hardy routine, Bell and Speakman's campaign—the line was eventually altered to 'The Way We Play'—won the day. Scali would keep the business.

Two months later, Bell was recruited by Judy Wallis, a headhunter, to become creative director at Saatchi & Saatchi. "I really felt I needed to know what I was capable of doing on my own," he says. "The appeal was the chance to test something that I had not really done to that extent, and that was to run a creative department."

The consequences of his move, however, were painful.

"To me the personal tragedy was that I lost a very dear friend in the process. Gary, from that moment that I resigned, refused to maintain the friendship. And we had a relationship that was enormously close. It hurt a great deal."

Exacerbating the hurt was the sad state of affairs at Saatchi & Saatchi. Bell thought he had been hired to "do terrific stuff." Instead, he ended up putting out fires. Accounts that were meant to be solid were in fact teetering. The first week on the job, three advertisers put their assignments up for review.

"You will never do great work unless it is the agency's mission to do great work," he says, regret colouring his words. "Everybody involved, from the president all the way through, has to make that commitment."

Peter Greene, then Saatchi & Saatchi's president, "talked the game, but that was not his commitment. The other part is Peter—bless his heart—I'm not terribly sure he knew what great work was. The deck was stacked against accomplishing that."

In 1990, when Bill Durnan, senior vice-president and national creative director at MacLaren, asked him if he would be interested in working for him as a senior writer, Bell didn't hesitate.

"My greatest strength is as a creator," he says. "It's what I'm best at, and what I love doing. That's why I went to MacLaren, because it was a chance to do exactly what I wanted to do, and have the freedom to do it."

He quit Saatchi & Saatchi and joined MacLaren to work on the Molson Breweries account.

Less than two months into the job, he was abruptly fired after being quoted in the press criticizing a Canadian Airlines ad. It left a wound that still aches.

"It never dawned on me that I would ever get fired. I always figured I'd pulled my weight. I worked like a son of a bitch. I hopefully worked smart. I'm not one of those guys who's ever going to get fired—and whack! It's like a Louisville Slugger across the forehead."

The public humiliation exacted a toll. "The ultimate lesson coming out of that was—and it took about a year to sink in—I will never again work for somebody. I will be in a partnership equity situation. I will never again go and draw a pay-cheque."

With that resolve, Bell turned down an offer from Michael Palmer, chairman of Toronto agency Bozell Palmer Bonner, to become creative director. Palmer could not offer shares in the company. Hayter, who Bell was also talking to at the time, could.

So he returned to Vickers & Benson for the third time in his career.

"I want to be a part of this," Bell says, looking out past his door to the agency beyond. "I want to be a part of the revitalization of this agency, which has been a home for me. It's the place I started. I came back to it, and here I am again. It's like a circle. All roads lead to Rome. In this case, all roads lead back to Vickers & Benson. So here I am."

Like Hayter and Bell, Jim Satterthwaite was not cut out for the academic life.

Born in post-war England to working-class parents, he led a quiet, if hard, life in the Midlands. "It was such a fucking struggle to make ends meet," he says. "People didn't have much, but the quality of life on the other hand was great. I look back and it was a lovely place to grow up as a kid."

What he hated, though, was the Catholic school he was forced to attend, the redundancy of Latin, the hypocrisy of the cane-wielding priests.

Then, when he was twelve, on a trip to visit American relatives in New Jersey, he had an epiphany.

"I'd never been anywhere. People didn't go to America in those days unless they were very rich. After seeing the struggle that everybody had to go through to survive, let alone thrive in Britain, I saw people simply applying themselves and working hard in America. I saw very ordinary people doing really well. It sounds superficially very materialistic, but it was a much more attractive society to me, I think, because it was a society where one was not encumbered by any kind of class system."

He returned to England, resolving to move to North America one day, this time to stay.

When he finished grammar school, he took some part-time courses at a community college in Birmingham. "I worked as a salesman while I did that, and during that year decided I'd like to try advertising," he says matter-of-factly about his entry into the business.

In 1963, at the age of seventeen, he read an ad for a trainee's position at a local agency, applied and was hired for three pounds a week. A year later, he started with a bigger agency at eight pounds.

Then it was off to London, to work in the ad department of the large appliance retailer Curry's. It was a dream job. He wrote and produced radio commercials and programs for the pirate stations that played the pop music of the day.

London was swinging, and Satterthwaite, then eighteen, was smack in the middle of all the action. All the big stars—Peter & Gordon, Georgie Fame, Freddy & The Dreamers—played his shows.

"These groups would basically do it for nearly nothing," he explains. "They'd do it for the promotion, the live exposure, to be on the radio."

Then one day he saw an ad in the *Daily Express.* "Canada, Land of Opportunity," it beckoned. Recalling his youthful visit to America, he decided to emigrate, with seventy-five dollars in his pocket. It was 1967, Centennial year.

He landed a job at J. Walter Thompson in the media department as an estimator.

"I worked incredibly hard, and I really enjoyed it. I viewed it as a creative opportunity. There were a lot of numbers and crunching and everything else, but whenever I had an opportunity to do some thinking and was given a job to do, I always tried to be creative about it."

Within a year he was promoted to supervisor. "Then John Hayter came on the scene from Spitzer Mills & Bates as an account executive on Alberto-Culver, which was the toughest account in the agency."

One of Hayter's innovations was a new-products think tank. "He'd give us a brief, and we'd come up with ideas for products. I used to phone him at home all the time, and drive him crazy. The phone would ring at 9:30 Sunday nights and his wife would say, 'John, it's that Jim again.'"

When Hayter joined Alberto-Culver, he hired Satterthwaite as an assistant product manager. After a couple of years, Satterthwaite decided he wanted back in the agency fold, so he joined Ogilvy & Mather as an executive on the Campbell Soup and Rowntree accounts. But he was put off by the agency's stuffy, buttoned-down culture. Still a bit brash and always the non-conformist, he was made to feel like an interloper. When Hayter called him about rejoining Alberto-Culver as marketing manager, he accepted.

He soon regretted his decision. "Selling shampoo I found really, really fucking boring. I got no satisfaction from it."

So he quit, and with his wife, Aldona, took off to see the world. They bought a Volkswagen camper and took off for fifteen months, through the United States, down into Mexico. At Panama, they got on a ship bound for Barcelona. They travelled through Europe, went to England to visit family, and returned to Canada.

Feeling recharged, he was ready for a long-term career opportunity. He joined McCann-Erickson in late 1973, assigned to the Chesebrough-Pond's account. It was the start of a sixteen-year relationship with the Interpublic Group, the New York-based conglomerate that owned McCann-Erickson.

Four years later, he started up Quadrant Advertising Ltd., a stand-alone subsidiary of McCann. It was set up to service accounts the larger agency couldn't handle because of conflicts. When Interpublic bought and merged ad agencies SSC&B and Lintas Worldwide, Quadrant became its Canadian arm. The newly configured agency prospered throughout the 1980s, handling accounts for Diet Coke, Nestlé and Speedy Muffler King among others. Billings rose to $50 million.

Then, in 1988, Interpublic bought and merged MacLaren Advertising with Satterthwaite's Lintas Canada. The deal put him out of a job. To soften the blow, he was offered the managing director's job of the Lintas operation in London, England. The family home was sold, the household goods packed and away they went.

Within three months, rumours began flying that the Lintas office was looking to merge with a local London firm. Satterthwaite couldn't believe it. Eight months later it was a done deal, and he was unemployed once more.

"I was probably clinically depressed by this point," he remembers, the bitterness still raw. "Aldona knew that I was unhappy. She could tell something was going on. And I didn't know how to deal with it. I didn't really tell her everything because I figured what is she going to do? Worry as much as me?"

Still shell-shocked, he got a call one day from a top executive from Interpublic's New York office, asking how everything was. "I immediately smell bullshit. He's a great guy, but I know this is not why he's phoning. It turns out the chairman of McCann-Erickson in Australia has collapsed and died of a heart attack, and would I like to go to Australia as chairman of McCann-Erickson?"

Satterthwaite was dumbfounded. He knew he didn't want to take the job, but agreed to consider it. He called back later to decline.

He had come to the realization that he was being used as a pawn in a global chess game. "Had I gone to Australia, done whatever you have to do, perhaps I would have become a castle or a bishop. Hey! This is great. Maybe I'll become the queen. But there's only one piece on that chess board which, when removed, ends the game. And that's the king. Do I want to be the king?

"I don't think so. I'm not that driven. My ambition is not that consuming. If you don't want to do that you can be just knocked off that board any time. I didn't want to be the victim of somebody saying 'I'll sacrifice that pawn to get that knight.' Which is basically what they'd done with me at MacLaren, what they'd done with me in the U.K. Why would I do this to myself? I decided I wanted to have more control over my own destiny."

He accepted a fat settlement from Interpublic, and moved back to

Toronto, wondering what his next step would be. While he bided his time, he took on some consulting work for Bramalea, the real-estate firm, and Harrison Young Pesonen & Newell, a media-buying agency.

"It was great, but I wasn't part of building anything, and I knew I wanted to. But I didn't know what. I analyzed all the agencies around to see which I'd like to work for."

At the time, Young & Rubicam was looking for a new president to replace Jim McCoubrey, who had left to join Telemedia Publishing Inc. Satterthwaite didn't really want the job, but persuaded himself otherwise. The stress of that decision was so intense he developed stomach pains. He couldn't sleep. When the Young & Rubicam recruiter guessed the truth, that Satterthwaite's commitment was wobbly, Satterthwaite welcomed the rejection with a tremendous sense of relief.

"I didn't have to do what was expected, or what I demanded of myself," he says, eyes brightening. "It was a turning point. You have few moments like that in your life."

But there was still the question of what to do with his life. He knew he didn't want to stay with consulting. "This was a way to make a few bucks, do something I enjoyed with people I liked. Be appreciated for what I did. Be thanked for what I did. Be respected for what I did. It helped me recharge my batteries and restore my dignity after being kicked around like a fucking football.

"I knew there would have to be something more. Which was when the phone rang one night. It was John Hayter."

They met on several occasions, and Hayter outlined to his former colleague what he wanted to do with Vickers & Benson. Satterthwaite got excited at the possibilities.

"I knew this was what I wanted to do. It gave me some control over my own destiny. I mean, we never have complete control over our own destiny. But some control. I was working with somebody I trusted in the only agency in the country that I'd identified that I really had an interest in being a part of."

Satterthwaite borrowed money to invest in the company, and became Hayter's second in command.

"I wanted an entrepreneurial opportunity, so you have to put your money on the line. You're going to Vegas. I gambled. I'm gambling today. I always will be as long as my money's in this company. But that's what you do. That's what I wanted, and that's what I got."

Philp is groping to find the right words to describe his new life as a creative director. Sure, it's a little scary changing career paths, he says. But it's more than that. Then he hits on the metaphor he's looking for and takes it for a spin.

"I'm an inveterate cyclist," he says. "I just love it, and I can't find enough time to do it."

He bikes to work every chance he gets. That's fine in the summer, when the days are long and the sun sets late, but as winter approaches and the days shorten, the thought of riding in the dark makes him skittish. He confronts his fears.

"The first couple of nights I rode home after dark it was almost primal. Danger was everywhere. Over your shoulders. On side streets. The mailboxes. You were constantly, completely focused on the here and now and the moment. Because if you didn't, if you let your mind wander and you made a mistake you're in the hospital. That's what this has been like too."

Not that he would change his lot for anything. He loves the rush of being in charge of the agency's creative output too much. And as far as he can tell, it makes perfect sense that he have that responsibility. He has always liked to ride solo.

He was born in the United States in the late 1950s, but grew up around London, Ontario, then as now a nice but provincial backwater. Philp was bored.

"I was not the best student in the world," he says sheepishly. "I was constantly getting report cards saying, 'Bruce is not living up to his potential.' But I liked drawing and I liked writing. So I ended up going to the advertising arts course that was offered by the community college."

He also took some marketing courses, but jobs in advertising were scarce. While he was working in a packaging company, a friend told him about a graphic design firm that was looking for sales reps. Philp applied and got the job.

With his college training, he eventually rose up the ladder to become head of marketing. But after more than four years, he realized that he wasn't going to go any higher. The top jobs were reserved for the designers and those with a stake in the company.

When Panasonic, one of the firm's clients, put the word out that they needed an assistant manager of advertising for their audio products division, Philp grabbed it. Nine months later he was manager of corporate relations and advertising.

"It was a great place—a really happening place—and the product was terrific," he says. Would have stayed there, too, but Panasonic began cutting its ad spending. Unfortunately, that didn't leave him much of a role.

"So sooner than I would have preferred I started casting about for a job at an agency."

He ended up at Schur Peppler, then a new agency set up by two admen, Jeff Schur and Dan Peppler, to take on the advertising for Honda. "I worked my ass off," Philp recalls. But at least his hard work got noticed. When Saatchi & Saatchi landed the rival Toyota account, they wanted to parachute people in who had experience in the Japanese car category. A headhunter came knocking, and Philp took the plunge.

But rather than be pigeonholed as a car man, Philp dropped Toyota to gain some packaged-goods experience. He worked on Ivory soap, Tylenol pain reliever and Oil of Olay. "It makes for a great résumé, because it was the number one imported car, number one bar of soap, the number one moisturizer and the number one pain reliever," he brags.

Then one day Terry Bell joined the agency as creative director. The two hit it off, becoming friends as well as colleagues. So Philp wasn't too surprised when Bell called him up after he joined Vickers & Benson to ask him if he would be interested in talking to Hayter about a job.

It was a tough decision. Philp says he thought it over "about four times before agreeing to come over."

"I analyzed it so many different ways. I think that in the end there were maybe three trump cards, things I couldn't rationally ignore. One was I think success at Saatchi would have eventually entailed leaving the country to work somewhere else."

But as a divorced father, that would mean leaving his children behind. No way, he decided.

"The second thing was the opportunity to work with Terry again. The third, the possibility of having a stake in an agency was very attractive."

Unlike Hayter, Satterthwaite and Bell, Philp didn't become a partner in Vickers & Benson when he joined, but the fact that it was even discussed was a tantalizing prospect.

Once again he trusted his instincts and took the plunge. Like the other newcomers, he soon realized Vickers & Benson was in dire need of a shake-up.

"I didn't feel particularly warmly welcomed," he says of his early encounters with the staff. "To say it was run like a family would be about right. There were a lot of Uncle so-and-sos and Aunt so-and-sos whose foibles were simply tolerated.

"I have a reputation for being a notorious tight ass, and the reason for that is I'm not naturally disciplined. So I taught myself to be that way to overcome the weakness. By the time I left Saatchi I pretty well had everything honed. I knew there was a right and wrong way to do things."

The sloppiness he found at Vickers & Benson was irksome. "It was tolerated, and I think in some unintentional and insidious way, encouraged."

The situation only began improving after Hurst was brought in to do a study of the place, Philp believes.

"He was Terry O'Malley's discovery. And it gave Terry O'Malley a seat at the table which he had not properly had up to that point," he says. "My sense of it was Terry was feeling pretty excluded."

Philp worries that is still the case. He casts his mind back to when he was interviewed by O'Malley prior to joining the agency.

"The theme of the whole conversation was, to my memory, how profoundly disappointed he was with everybody in business in general. How people don't honour commitments any more. They don't keep promises. Personal loyalties don't matter as much as solving the next problem does.

"I came away feeling like I had spent time with a man who was pretty—I won't say bitter—but a bit disappointed with the whole thing."

# CHAPTER 11

O'MALLEY IS IN his fifth-floor sanctuary, musing about his future. He knows full well that he is the author of his own predicament. But is there anything he can really do about it? Or wants to do about it?

It wasn't supposed to turn out this way. He was meant to be long gone, perhaps running for elected office in his hometown of St. Catharines. Or maybe getting involved in the winery business.

"John is convinced that I can't live without Vickers & Benson, and that I just won't exist without coming here everyday," he says softly, conspiringly.

Well, is he right?

"I don't know," he answers, shrugging. "I don't think so. I'm not an ego-driven guy." Remarkably, he says this with a straight face.

"I guess where the frustration is for me now is that some of these opportunities, whatever they might be, are drifting by me. They're quite idealistic in a sense. I don't feel old at all. I feel quite vital. But chronologically I think, 'Shit, I better get going here.'"

His hands are shaking ever so slightly. "You get to a point where you want freedom," he says. "I don't want to worry any more. You can't imagine the amount of worry. It's just endless."

The years of strain suddenly seem to buckle his resolve. The relentless responsibility to meet payrolls. The concern about co-workers, about clients.

"We never had the luxury of a rich uncle in New York or Chicago or London," he says, the old fire flashing. The multinationals worry about losing accounts. He has to worry about losing his company. In a new-business presentation, they could say, "Here's a great idea. You're going to love it."

And him? "You're saying, 'Here's a great idea. You've got to love it because we need the business.'"

For all that, Vickers & Benson will survive and prosper, he says. The agency's core strengths—flexibility, superior thinking and multidisciplinary skills—are still intact.

"For the time being, and until things change, I'm the ultimate scorecard," he declares. "I either like or don't like what's going on."

And if he doesn't like it, he is prepared to lay down the law. His ownership position gives him that right. He has not exercised it to date, but will to protect his investment.

He is saddened that Vickers & Benson failed to get the Shoppers account, because it would have shown the rightness of the agency's new direction. It could have been a defining moment, just as winning McDonald's was in the 1970s.

"I was hoping, much less from a business sense but more from just a psychological sense, that yeah, they did land it. The core thinking works."

But life is seldom that poetic.

"This business demands enormous resilience. Even when you win you don't win. You tie. Most clients will never suggest it could be the advertising. If it's all going well it's because they've got good people, good products, distribution or whatever. And if it's going rotten? We better change the agency."

His face brightens.

"I'm encouraged. I'm looking forward to the next generation. Vickers & Benson is hopefully an infinite relay race that just keeps on going with great athletes in every generation. It's gone from Rex and Don, through to Bryan and his guys, through to Bill and me. And now John. It's pretty unique in that way.

"We're old by years, but I'll tell you, the work is really good. It's never been bad. It's always been good, really good or outstanding. I've always said the longer you're in it, the better you get at it. Advertising is peaks and valleys. You just keep pushing the standard up."

One floor up and another world away in his executive corner suite, Hayter contemplates the question of O'Malley's role with the agency.

"Terry O'Malley was Vickers & Benson. Terry O'Malley is now the father figure of Vickers & Benson. And as the father figure he will be absolutely key and important to the company."

Hurst had referred to it as a kind of corporate mythology. Hayter likes the metaphor. Turns it over and over in his mind like a multifaceted jewel.

It makes sense to him that whatever "Vickers & Benson" stands for— the culture, the personality, the aspirations, whatever one cares to label it—O'Malley has come to embody it as the present-day custodian in a long line of custodians.

Make no mistake: There is no going back to the old ways. "We floated,"

Hayter says. "But we can't operate that way any more. Everybody has to know that there's a new leader in Bruce Philp in the creative department, that our long-ball hitters report to him. And Terry may be one of those long-ball hitters, if that's what he wants to be."

The problem, he says, is that O'Malley was over-stretched. He was the executive creative director and the business manager. He remains the largest shareholder. It was enough to burn anybody out.

Hayter reverts to the familiarity of a sports analogy like a ballplayer to his worn catcher's mitt.

"Why do you have your best performers in the dugout, playing the game and up in the head office and trying to manage it? You don't do it in sports. Why would you do it in this business? This business needs stars. It has a hierarchy of stars. It doesn't mean that you're not important.

"They should be on the field, not doing administrivia, which they hate and are bad at. If they do it long enough they become frustrated and unproductive amd eventually leave or go away."

But while O'Malley ruminates, Hayter already knows what he must do.

"I have to create the energy in the place," he says, pumping himself up. "I have to create focus for where our big client opportunities are. I have to create focus where we can make a difference."

He knows it won't be easy.

"Some people will absolutely disagree with us. Change is difficult, and this has been a company that has not had a lot of change. And when you do something that will appear to be as outrageous as we're doing they'll think we've lost it. And I don't mean to brand people who have been here a long time. We've got to keep in mind it took us months to get here, if not two years to get here.

"We were duking it out in the boardroom a couple of months ago. We shouldn't expect them to embrace it on day one. So it's up to us to make them feel comfortable, so there is the buy-in and the support."

And as he begins to spend more time with the staff, away from simply managing "the business of the business," it will eventually wear down the walls that separate the camps, Hayter believes.

"We're moving away from being a family to being a team. It's necessary because you can no longer run a business in today's climate on a family basis. Family, unfortunately, is not demanding enough of one another. Too often we can excuse and cover up and say it's okay. The core family values, of course, are important to keep. But today's marketplace requires that we play at a different level.

"The team plays together, works together and is demanding of one another. We have expectations of the roles each of us plays, and we ask that each person play to those expectations. As a team, we're interdependent upon one another and as we push one another's skills, we will get better and better and better."

If he has a model, it is his favourite burger client.

"McDonald's do a lot of things wrong. But they don't bullshit themselves. They keep pushing and pushing and pushing one another until they get it right. And I think there's a lot of that in me, and in other people here."

The process of change the agency had started was only the beginning of a long march to the horizon.

"Our mission statement, where we say 'People given the power to make things happen' will really come to life. Because they will be given the power. It has not been a reality to date because we have round pegs in square holes. And we haven't had the lubrication, the uplifting leadership. We've all been doing it in different levels and different spots, sending confusing messages. All that's eliminated."

His confidence is messianic.

"I think in every organization you need a dozen people who will drive the company. Then you need another 50 per cent of the company to really feel passionate about it. Then you need a lot of dedicated people who respect the company and like their jobs and want to deliver. They aren't necessarily the creators or the masterminds, but they are inspired by what they see. We have to think of ourselves as winners, people that step up and compete at any level. And love it. Relish it. Go for it."

He settles back in his blue velvet chair. Takes a sip of Perrier. Dreams the possibilities.

# INDEX